INDIA

INDIA

IMPRESSIONS AND SUGGESTIONS

J. KEIR HARDIE, M. P.

GYAN

Published by

GYAN

Gyan Publishing House
5, Ansari Road
Daryaganj, New Delhi-110002
Phone: 011-47034999, 9811692060
E-mail: books@gyanbooks.com

Distribution Network
gyanbooks.com
India, USA, Canada, UK, Australia, France

ISBN: 978-81-212-8644-2 (PB)
First Published, 1909

2nd Impression 2023

Printed at: Gyan Press, Delhi.

INDIA
Author: J. KEIR HARDIE

INDIA

INDIA

IMPRESSIONS AND SUGGESTIONS

BY

J. KEIR HARDIE, M.P.

[*SECOND EDITION*]

LONDON:
INDEPENDENT LABOUR PARTY,
23, BRIDE LANE, E.C.

1909.

DEDICATED

WITH RESPECT,

TO THE MEMORY OF THE LATE

RAI BAHADUR SURJA KANTA ACHARYA,

MAHARAJA OF MYMENSINGH,

A WISE COUNSELLOR, AND A PATRIOTIC LOVER

OF THE

MOTHERLAND,

TO THE TRADITION OF WHOSE GREAT PAST HIS

LIFE ADDED A FRESH LUSTRE.

CONTENTS

If I were to look over the whole world to find out the country most richly endowed with all the wealth, power, and beauty that nature can bestow —in some parts a very paradise on earth—I should point to India. If I were asked under what sky the human mind has most fully developed some of its choicest gifts, has most deeply pondered on the greatest problems of life, and has found solutions of some of them which well deserve the attention even of those who have studied Plato and Kant— I should point to India. And if I were to ask myself from what literature we here in Europe, we who have been nurtured almost exclusively on the thoughts of Greeks and Romans, and of one Semitic race, the Jewish, may draw that corrective which is most wanted in order to make our inner life more perfect, more comprehensive, more universal, in fact, more truly human, a life not for this life only, but a transfigured and eternal life— again I should point to India.

MAX MÜLLER.

PREFACE.

WHILST travelling in India in 1907, I contributed a series of letters to the *Labour Leader*, and these form the basis of the following chapters. That this method of writing has its drawbacks I know, but there are also some compensating advantages. Impressions recorded while they are warm are more virile than when laboriously compiled out of stale memories.

India and its affairs are now exciting a great deal of interest, and it is owing to that fact that this little volume sees the light. I have neither claim nor desire to pose as an authority on India and its affairs, but two months spent in the country during which every minute was occupied either in travelling or in interviewing officials or representative men of all stations in life and of all creeds, castes, and classes, led me to certain conclusions. These, with the reasons which led to their being formed, will be found set forth in what follows.

Much controversy has arisen over the question as to whether the condition of the people of India, especially the peasantry, has improved or deteriorated during the past one hundred and fifty years. Many contradictory statements of missionaries, traders, travellers, and officials have been quoted for and against. One quotation from an official document dated 1833 which I have seen given as an evidence of the benefits which British rule has brought is curious, and worth reproducing here as showing how progress and improvement presents itself to certain minds:—

"Labourers," wrote the official who compiled the report, "whom nothing would have induced to work more than six hours in twenty-four (under native rule), and who often declined to work at all on a cloudy day, were willing to toil from sunrise to sunset" (under British rule).

This would be amusing were it not that it is seriously advanced as a proof of the blessings which our rule has brought to the peasants of India.

Whether for ultimate good or ill, we have entirely changed the conditions under which the people of India had lived for at least twenty-five hundred years prior to European occupation. Take, for example, the method of holding the land and the method of raising the revenue. The *Encyclopædia Britannica*, in its article on India, says that Akbar, the great and wise Mohammedan ruler, fixed the revenue from land at one-third the total produce. It was paid in kind, and here is how it was collected:—

> The land was not held by private owners, but by occupiers under the petty corporation (village panchayet). The revenue was not due from individuals, but from the community represented by its headman. The aggregate harvest of the village fields was thrown into a common fund, and before the general

> distribution the headman was bound to set aside the share of the state. No other system could be theoretically more just or in practice less obnoxious to the people.

That method at least has disappeared, and now each individual cultivator of land has to pay his revenue direct, not as a collective part of the harvest yield, but as an individual rent for the particular piece of land he himself cultivates, and this has to be paid in coin and not in grain as formerly. This is a revolutionary change and one which I believe is playing havoc with the people.

The term "famine in India" is a misnomer. There are times and seasons when famine is spread over great areas affecting many millions of people, but at the same time in other parts of the country sufficient grain is being exported to feed all who are hungry if only it did not pay better to send it abroad. Thus, according to the Famine Comsioners' Report upon the great famine of 1877-8, when scores of millions of people in Southern India were starving and five millions two hundred and twenty thousand (5,220,000) actually died of hunger, over sixteen million hundredweights (16,000,000 cwts.) of rice were exported from Calcutta to foreign lands. This illustrates what happens in connection with every so-called famine in India.

That there is discontent in India is not to be denied. What is denied by the officials and the army of ex-officials and hangers-on in London is that there is any legitimate grievance to justify agitation. To these I commend the opinion of Lord Cromer, who, addressing his fellow-peers in the House of Lords on a recent occasion, said:—

> The position of India at the present time is almost unique. It is, so far as I know, the only important country in the world where education has considerably advanced, which is governed in all essential particulars by non-resident foreigners. It is also the only country where the Civil Service in all its higher administrative branches is in the hands of aliens appointed by a foreign country under stringent educational tests.

Those who are so prone to denounce all Indian reformers as seditious malcontents may find food for reflection in Lord Cromer's words.

In 1858, at the close of the great mutiny, the late Queen Victoria, in the healing manifesto which she issued to the people of India, said:—

> It is our will that, so far as may be, our subjects, of whatever race or creed, be fully and impartially admitted to offices in our service, the duties of which they may be qualified by their education, ability, and integrity duly to discharge.

The pages which follow will give some idea how this solemn pledge was kept. Then in 1908, fifty years after, King Edward, in the jubilee proclamation, used almost identical language:—

> Steps are being continually taken towards obliterating distinctions of race as the test for access to posts of public authority and power. In this path I confidently expect and intend the progress henceforward to be steadfast and sure, as education spreads, experience ripens, and the lessons of responsibility are well-learned by the keen intelligence and apt capabilities of India.

If the pledge of Queen Victoria had been carried out the language of the second proclamation would not have been that of repetition of a promise but that of credit for the fulfilment of a royal undertaking given fifty years before. What sincerity lies behind the second pledge time will show.

The difficulty in the way of introducing political reforms is alleged to be in the main due to difference of race, caste, and creed. These difficulties are more imaginary than real, and I have shown how they have been and are being overcome in the more progressive of the native states. The two main divisions of population are Hindus and Mohammedans. Out of a population of say 300,000,000 the Mohammedans muster about 60,000,000, of whom only some hundreds of thousands are Mughals or Pathans, who came in as invaders and conquerors. Most of the rest of the Mussulman population are Hindus who have been converted to Mohammedanism, many of them in the olden days at the point of the sword. The Mussulmans predominate in the north, but when the Punjab is left behind it is rarely that a Mughal is seen, though when he is there is no mistaking him because of his superior physique and proud, erect bearing. Among the peasantry, Hindu and Mohammedan, belonging as they do to the same race, mingle freely, attend each other's religious festivals and social functions, and when left alone behave as good neighbours should. The policy now being pursued by the Government is to show special favour to the Mohammedans, and it looks with a complacent eye upon, even if it does nothing to foster, outbursts of fanatical strife between the two sections of religious belief. Great Britain may one day have to pay a long price for this folly. The Mussulmans are a warlike people come of a conquering race. They are united by ties of religion rather than nationality, and as there are two hundred millions of them in the world they may one day take it into their heads to try once again to win supreme power for Allah in the East.

I am fully conscious of the many imperfections which the following pages contain. That the book will excite criticism goes without saying. That I shall welcome. Everything which serves to call attention to the condition of India and its peoples must be of advantage to the patient toilers and thinkers of that far-off land, for the well-being of whose suffering millions the democracy of Great Britain are now responsible.

J. K. H.

May, 1909.

INDIA,

IMPRESSIONS AND SUGGESTIONS.

SOME FACTS AND FIGURES.

THE old tradition which associated India with unlimited wealth still lingers. One hundred years ago, when trade and plunder were transforming certain middle class families into millionaire nabobs, everyone was talking about it. We hear less now-a-days about India's great wealth or about the great fortunes which merchant princes have been able to accumulate there, but at no period of India's history has there ever been such a regular soaking drain upon its people as now. It is calculated that the British capital invested in India in railways, irrigation schemes, public works, and undertakings of various kinds amounts to £500,000,000. That, of itself, at 5 per cent. interest, represents a burden upon India of £25,000,000 sterling a year. By a burden I mean that the interest is paid to bondholders in this country and is not, therefore, benefiting the people from whom it is taken. Then, in addition, there are civil and military pensions and other items, so that the estimate of £30,000,000 a year made by Mr. A. J. Wilson, of the *Investors' Review*, is certainly well within the mark. Eighty per cent. of the taxes in India are raised by revenue assessment upon land. The Government steadily discourages private ownership in land as it objects to an idle landlord class coming between itself and the real producers of wealth—those who till the soil. The amount of taxes raised direct from the peasant is from 50 per cent. to 65 per cent. of the value of the yield of the land, in addition to which they have to pay local cesses and various other small items, so that probably not less than 75 per cent. of the harvest goes in taxes. To most people this will seem incomprehensible. A 5 per cent. tax on income at home leads to heavy and continuous grumbling, and yet the 5 per cent. is assessed not on the total produce of the land, but on the profits. What, then, must be the condition of a country in which the tax is not 5 per cent. on the profits, but 75 per cent. on the harvest reaped? From time to time the revenue charges are revised so that the Government may obtain the last penny which can be wrung from the over-weighted peasant. Increases of 30 per cent. are common, and there are many on record of 50, 70, and even 100 per cent. It is this fact which keeps the people of India in a condition of perpetual, hopeless, grinding poverty. It is commonly alleged that the peasant under British rule pays less than he formerly did under native rule. This statement can be refuted in a variety of ways, but here are some figures which at least are fairly conclusive on the point. When the Province of Bombay came under British dominion in 1817, the revenue claimed by its rulers from the peasants was estimated at 8,000,000 rupees. The method of assessment was to take one-fourth of the crop as it stood, good and bad alike. Thus in years of plenty Government and people alike benefited, whilst in lean years both suffered. Now a fixed yearly sum is charged, be the crop good, bad, or indifferent. Immediately after 1817 a process of forcing up the revenue was begun, and in 1823 it had been increased to 15,000,000 rupees, and in 1875 to 48,000,000 rupees. When Sir Thomas Munro was appointed Governor of Madras early last century a similar forcing process had been at work, and after a thorough investigation into the complaints which were reaching him from all sides as to people dying of starvation owing to the heavy land assessment, so convinced was he of the extortion of the Government demands that he ordered an immediate reduction of 25 per cent. to be made. The officials under him at first refused to carry out his order, but he was not a man to be trifled with, and in the end they had to submit. The outcome of this continuous extortion is that the people are reduced to such a condition of abject destitution as is probably not to be equalled in any other country in the world, and certainly not in one which for a hundred years has been under civilised rule. Sir William Hunter, who was Director-General of Indian Statistics, and who loved India and its people, put it on record that forty millions of the people never at any time had enough to eat; and Mr. S. S. Thorburn, Financial Commissioner of the

Punjab, declared that "seventy millions of Indian peasants are in such a condition of hopeless poverty that no reforms can do them any good." Testimony of a similar kind could be multiplied indefinitely. In further support of this contention I will quote the names of three living authorities, neither of whom will be accused of having undue sympathy with the natives. In 1882 Lord Cromer, as he now is, declared that the national income of India worked out at 36s. per head of the population. Lord George Hamilton, in 1894, whilst he was Secretary of State for India, gave the average at £2, and this was endorsed by Lord Curzon, who, in reply to some figures showing a lower estimate, proudly declared that the income of the peasantry averaged £1 6s. 8d. per head per annum. Other estimates, only quasi-official, put the income of the peasant as low as 12s. 6d. per head. As showing what this means, I may note that in Great Britain the average income is £42 per head, and that even in agricultural Russia it is £11. These figures speak for themselves. One of the glaring injustices in connection with the administration of India is the way in which qualified Indians are shut out from the higher paid posts in the Civil Service. Dr. Jabez Sunderland, an American authority, is responsible for the statement that 8,000 European Anglo-Indian officials draw yearly salaries totalling £13,930,554, whilst 130,000 native Indians, also included in the Civil Service, receive only £3,284,163. If it be alleged that this is due to the superior ability of the European official, then I can only reply that all the facts are against such an assumption.

What we have done for education in India is another boast frequently heard. Here, also, so far at least as the older provinces of India are concerned, the boast is ill-founded. The total number of children attending schools in the whole of India, including the native states, is only about five millions, and the cost which the Government of India spends upon education works out at about 1½d. per head. The military expenditure, I may add in passing, averages 1s. per head of the population. Max Müller, on the strength of official documents and a missionary report concerning education in Bengal prior to the British occupation, asserts that there were then 80,000 native schools in Bengal, or one for every 400 of the population. Ludlow, in his history of British India, says that "in every Hindoo village which has retained its old form I am assured that the children generally are able to read, write, and cipher, but where we have swept away the village system as in Bengal there the village school has also disappeared." That, I think, disposes effectively of the boast that we are *beginning* to give education to the people of India.

Here is Sir Thomas Munro's testimony of what India was in the days prior to British occupation :

> If a good system of agriculture, unrivalled manufacturing skill, a capacity to produce whatever can contribute to either convenience or luxury, schools established in every village for teaching reading, writing and arithmetic, the general practice of hospitality and charity among each other, and, above all, a treatment of the female sex full of confidence, respect and delicacy, are among the signs which denote a civilised people—

> then the Hindus are not inferior to the nations of Europe; and if civilisation is to become an article of trade between England and India, I am convinced that England will gain by the import cargo.

We are too apt to forget that civilisation had blossomed in India ere its rudiments had begun to sprout in Europe. A people with a past which has shed enlightenment upon religion, art, science, and literature in every country in the world is surely entitled to different treatment from that meted out to half-developed savages; and yet our whole system of government in India rests upon the assumption that its people are either unfit or unworthy to be trusted with even the semblance of self-government. It is that which galls the mind and sears the heart of this cultured and refined people.

CALCUTTA.

CALCUTTA on a Sunday afternoon in September is not a pleasant place. The heat is stifling, the European quarters are deserted, the Government of India is away at Simla, the summer capital of India, 1,100 miles from Calcutta, and 7,000 feet up in the mountains, where the air is cool and bracing and the snow-clad heights of the Himalayas are always in view. The few white men one sees wear a terribly bored, washed-out expression. The buildings are dank and dingy, and their interiors dusty and grimy. Altogether my first impression of the capital of India was that it was a most desirable place to get away from.

The sail up the Hoogly had been very interesting. The native villages lining the banks, the people in their bright-hued garments, the naked children running about the river banks or disporting themselves like young purpoises in the water; the passing of the quicksands, especially the James and Mary, where the lead is cast every minute, and where a big passenger steamer touched and was engulfed a few years ago—these and the many other new sights and sounds made the time pass pleasantly enough. There was also Trixie, the captain's little silken-haired terrier, and Tom Smith, his cat, which was the size of a well-grown lamb. When everything else failed, these were always in evidence.

I had not announced my coming, and so got in unnoticed, though a smart-witted journalist soon got on my track, and next day the news found its way into the press, and from then until I left the city there was not a single minute, from 6.30 in the morning until near midnight, when there was not some caller or deputation waiting for an interview. The patient way in which these men come and sit for hours waiting their turn to be seen or heard strikes the freshman as something quite new. A tall, well-formed Mohammedan, yclept Sheik Abdul, had attached himself to me as my personal servant, and no man was ever better or more intelligently looked after. He regulated the visitors, attended me at meals, slept outside the door to guard the room against unwary intruders, and all for 1s. 4d. a day. He would gladly have taken half that sum had anyone been mean enough to offer it. A young engineer, whom I had known in Manchester, and who was in business for himself in Calcutta, turned up, and volunteered his services as guide and private secretary, and right zealously did he perform his self-imposed task. He subsequently travelled with me as far as Lahore and Simla, and never once lost his cheerfulness, even under the most trying outbursts of a somewhat irascible temper. Quite a number of old friends from Dundee, Arbroath, and round Manchester way came to crack about old times. They were mostly employed in the jute and cotton mills. Their lot is not a pleasant one.

After dinner on Sunday evening I hired a gharry for a drive through the native quarter of the city, and found that full of interest. The shops, well stocked and open to the street, and with the merchant sitting cross-legged or reclining full length on the floor, lazily smoking from a hubble-bubble pipe, with a cocoanut for a bowl, and a small charcoal brazier atop the tobacco to keep it alight; heifers, goats, and pariah dogs going about scavenging for a meal; the electric cars, the gharries and broughams, the latter with two men on the box and two footmen standing behind, the slow-moving bullock carts, with their creaking, lumbering solid wheels; the clanging of the car and carriage bells, the constant shouting of drivers and others, the occasional glimpse of a carefully-closed palanquin, swung from long bamboo poles, borne aloft on the shoulders of four sturdy bearers; the weird, raucous music from the upper storeys of houses of doubtful fame—all these, together with the moving stream of people in their flowing white garments which crowded the dirty, ill-kept footpaths and streets, made up a kaleidoscopic panorama which might have been taken bodily from the pages of the Arabian Nights.

Everyone—European and Indian alike—strongly advised me to visit East Bengal. The partition of Bengal, to which I shall revert later, had led to a widespread agitation, which, in turn, led to the issue of an ordinance prohibiting public meetings, unless the sanction of the police had been first obtained. There were reported riots, murders, preaching of sedition, and a state of chaos generally. And so, as I had gone to India to study the causes of the unrest and its extent, I felt that East Bengal was a place I must visit. A week, I learned, was the shortest possible time in which the principal centres of the unrest could be visited, and I decided on giving at least that time to it. My travelling companion was Mr. Jagesh Chowdhuri, a barrister-at-law, who was educated at Oxford, and is now practising in Calcutta. He is editor of a legal weekly paper, and belongs to the moderate section of the Reform Party. He served a three years' term as a member of the Legislative Council of Bengal, where he represented his native district, and on which he earned considerable distinction. I invite attention to these details because of what afterwards happened to him during our visit to East Bengal.

During the two following days I had interviews with many influential and representative people, and soon became convinced that the feeling of irritation begotten by the partition of Bengal was not confined to any one section or class of the community. The heads of business firms, noblemen of distinction and high social standing, retired judges of the High Court, wealthy bankers, university professors, and others of like position all concurred in saying that Lord Curzon's autocratic method of forcing his undigested and ill-advised scheme of partition upon the province in the teeth of the opposition of practically the entire population, had been a great blunder, and that there could be no peace until it had been rectified in one form or another. Nor was this feeling confined to Indians. There are four Anglo-Indian daily newspapers—owned and staffed by Britishers—and of these, two opposed the partition. In the hotel where I put up, were men who had been in India for varying periods of years—from five to thirty—and each of these with whom I conversed, thought partition a mistake. I gained the impression that partition had no friends outside the hide-bound official element and the semi-official and reactionary press. I learned differently later; but that I will deal with in due course.

One thing which surprised me was the frank unaffected way in which the Indian gentlemen expressed themselves. I was a stranger to them in all but name and reputation; but had I been a bosom confidant of twenty years' standing they could not have spoken with less reserve. Professor Wilson, in his edition of Mill's *History of British India*, after a long and varied experience of the Hindu people, said: " So far from there being any servility there was extreme frankness, and I should say that where there is confidence without fear, frankness is one of the most universal features to the Indian character." My own experience entirely confirmed this judgment. Few of the men I am now referring to were taking any part in the anti-partition agitation, and all of them deplored much that was being done in connection therewith, but they one and all felt that they had been affronted, especially in that not one of them, not any Hindu of standing, so far as I could learn, had been consulted beforehand. " Why will not the English trust us—we that have served them so loyally and so well?" was the burden of their plaint. " Formerly there were some comings and goings between us; now they have opened a gulf, and every year they are widening it." The longer I remained in India the more convinced did I become of the truth of this. The colour line is being more rigidly drawn each year. " 'Tis true, 'tis pity, pity 'tis 'tis true."

EASTERN BENGAL.

From Calcutta to Goalundo is a run of just over 150 miles. The country, as seen from the train, is flat, and in places swampy. Water abounds, and so jute and paddy (rice) grow well, as do also sugar-cane, betel nut, and cocoanut. Clumps of palm trees dot the landscape, affording shelter to the villages. Occasionally a peasant is seen ploughing a mud hole with a pair of oxen yoked to a very primitive plough, he and his oxen wading ankle deep in the mud, which is the soil in which the paddy flourishes. Pools of water abound, and within these black buffaloes wallow, with only the ridge of their spine and their nostrils above the surface. In these same pools scores of men and boys are at work, soaking the jute, preparatory to stripping the fibre from the stock. After it has been stripped it is made up into bundles, sometimes drummed, sometimes loose, and is then ready for the market. Jute had paid so well for two years that much of the land formerly under rice was given over to jute, which had had a considerable effect on the price of food. In some cases one crop of jute and another of paddy was being raised from the same land; and where plenty of manure can be got, this pays exceedingly well.

At Gaolundo we left the train and embarked on one of the river steamers which are developing such an enormous trade through East Bengal and Assam. The soil is flat and alluvial, and the rivers are often miles in width, and in the rainy season, when they come down in tremendous floods, they re-shape the country through which they flow. Sometimes great stretches of land, and the villages on it, are swept away, new islands are formed, and when the floods are over the bed of the river may be found to have shifted several miles from its former course.

All along the banks villages are to be seen with people busy at work. The land is very flat, being the delta formed by the Ganges and Brahmasputra rivers, with their tributaries, on their way to the sea. Owing to the nature of the soil through which the rivers flow, the water is of a clayey hue, and I was informed that the people are dependent upon it for domestic use.

I confess I should not like to be reduced to the necessity of drinking from this source. It appears, however, that there are compensations for every drawback, and the muddy water of the Ganges is held to be an excellent remedy for indigestion. This is consoling, though to an Indian forced to live on a handful of rice a day, one has the feeling that indigestion is not likely to be a very acute source of trouble.

As the shades of evening drew on a great search-light from the prow of the boat suddenly flashed out into the darkness. It swept the river and the banks on each side, and then appeared a wondrous sight; thousands of flies came sailing down the stream of white light, and madly dashed themselves against the glass; some of them were as large as an ordinary sparrow at home, and I have seldom seen anything more beautiful than the flashing of their apparently transparent bodies as they skimmed gracefully through the air.

At length we reached the landing-stage for Serajganj, where we found a gaily-decorated house-boat, with several smaller craft, including the inevitable police boat, waiting to receive us. Many of the leading inhabitants were there. Serajganj itself is built on the banks of a small river, about four miles up from the landing place; and it took us just over three hours to reach the town. Wind and tide were against us, and the crew of the houseboat proved altogether inadequate for their task. I had heard and read much concerning the "seditious" song Bande Mataram, and was therefore only too pleased when a gentleman present consented to sing it. He had a beautiful voice, and accompanied himself on an accordion harmonium. The tune, as I heard it, was a weird wailing chant, with nothing so far as I could discover of a revolutionary nature about it. The song was composed some thirty years ago by a Bengali poet. It is an invocation to the spirit of the Motherland, and it is only of late that jaundiced pressmen and easily-deluded officials have come to regard it as "seditious." Here is what I understand is a fair translation, by a British Civil servant, the late Mr. W. H. Lee:—

My Motherland I sing,
  Her splendid streams, her glorious trees,
The zephyr from the far-off Vindyan heights,
  Her fields of waving corn,
The rapturous radiance of her moonlit nights,
  The trees in flower that flame afar,
The smiling days that sweetly vocal are,
  The happy, blessed Motherland!
Her will by seventy million throats extolled,
  Her power twice seventy million arms uphold;
Her strength let no man scorn.
  Thou art my head, thou art my heart,
My life and soul art thou,
  My song, my worship and my art
Before thy feet I bow,
  As Durga, scourge of all thy foes,
As Lakshmi, bowered in the flower
  That in the water grows,
As Bani, wisdom, power;
  The source of all our might,
Our every temple doth thy form unfold—
  Unequalled, tender, happy, pure,
Of splendid streams, of glorious trees,
  My Motherland I sing,
The stainless charms that e'er endure,
  And verdant banks and wholesome breeze,
That with her praises ring.

At Serajganj I experienced my first garlanding. It is an old-time custom of India to hang garlands of flowers round the neck of visitors and others, present them with gifts and fruit, and also to pelt them with flower petals, much as rice is thrown at a wedding party at home. Occasionally, the visitor is sprinkled with perfume, and on one occasion, in the south, gold-dust was used.

An Anglo-Indian pressman, in describing this garlanding, tried to make the flesh of his readers in Great Britain creep by telling them that most of the garlands with which I was garlanded in East Bengal were composed of marigolds, and that those who remembered the chapatis of the Mutiny period would know the significance which attached to this. Now, as a matter of fact, I was garlanded scores of times in India, but I never once saw a marigold among the flowers, certainly not in Bengal, nor could I find anyone who knew the inner meaning of this esotoric reference to marigolds, chapatis, and the Mutiny. So far as I could make out, the insinuation was only part of that campaign of lies with which a section of the Press sought to distort everything connected with my visit.

The garlanding is a bit trying to a modest man; but what could one do? One old man with gentle eyes said simply, as with trembling hands he placed the floral tribute round my neck, "This is our method of showing respect to those we love." Later on, and whilst travelling in other parts of the continent, the railway carriage was literally filled with similar tributes and offerings.

When we finally reached Serajganj I was conducted to the dak bungalow. These are rest-houses built by the local authorities, and used by officials and passing travellers, who are expected to provide their own bedding. The accommodation is ridiculously cheap, and good food can be had at moderate prices. The dak bungalow is an excellent institution, which I patronised as often as circumstances would permit.

Next morning we visited schools and colleges, and were interviewed by deputations. An incident connected with the higher-grade private schools here gives an illustration of the way in which British justice is upheld in this part of India. Some youths, it was alleged, had thrown mud at one of the local officials. The popular version of the story was that they were provoked into this by the official hitting out at them with his whip as he was riding past. Be this as it may, suspicion fell upon the boys of the high schools, of which there are two belonging to private individuals, and an order was issued that unless the boys were discovered and handed over to justice, the Government grant would be stopped. This punitive measure was carried out, and then another step was taken. A certain number of free scholarships were allocated to these schools each year, the boys who received them being entitled to a maintenance grant at the university. Intimation was sent to the school authorities that unless the culprits were discovered these free grants would be stopped; and a further step was threatened, and finally put into execution—that all the boys attending these schools would be prohibited from sitting for examination for entrance to the university.

All these punishments were in force at the time of my visit. Let an ordinary British reader look at the matter as it stands. Some boys, it is alleged, throw mud at a man riding past on horseback; the police are unable to discover who the culprits are; there are two efficient and well-conducted secondary schools carried on by public-spirited citizens in the village, and upon these is placed the responsibility of doing what the police, whose duty it is, fail to do—viz., locate the culprits and hand them over to justice; and for failing to do this police work the schools are punished in the way described above. I mention this incident in passing as an instance of how the Government encourages those who are seeking to promote education, and of how British dignity is upheld in East Bengal.

I had also at Serajganj my first personal illustration of the spirit with which the Indian is treated by his official rulers. Let me frankly say at the outset that it was an extreme case, but only differed in its extremeness from what is only too common throughout the greater part of India.

The facts are these: I was about to visit a prison, and was waiting, outside the gates, the arrival of the magistrate who was to accompany me. With me were some local gentlemen, amongst whom was also Mr. J. Chowdhuri, the Calcutta gentleman to whom I have already referred. My friends were all in native dress, though each of them was a man of some standing and social position, all having received a university education, and some of them having taken degrees at Cambridge and Oxford. To really understand what happened, let it be borne in mind that we were standing outside the prison walls; we were not within any fence or enclosure, but on a pathway running through an open field and leading to the prison gate. When the local magistrate came up to the spot I stepped out from my group of friends to meet him, and after conversing with him for a minute or so we were about to proceed towards the prison gate when he suddenly wheeled round, and speaking in the tone used by a half-caste warder when giving orders to the native prisoners, he shouted—specially directing his words and pointing to Mr. Chowdhuri—"Get out of the prison compound." The tone and the manner of the man were offensive in the extreme, and Mr. Chowdhuri smilingly suggested that he should not speak in that manner to him, as he was doing no harm. This only seemed to enrage the magistrate, and he kept shouting at intervals of about twenty seconds: "Get out of the prison compound; the public road is your place."

Mr. Chowdhuri explained to him who he was; that he had held a seat in the Provincial Legislative Council, and so on. But this only seemed to make the irate magistrate more angry, and he still kept shouting, until my friends, trembling and flushed with indignation, moved away towards the main road. My feelings were those of shame and humiliation at the scene I had witnessed. After the Indian gentlemen had gone, the magistrate following them with his eyes until they were back on to the main road, he turned to me and said that we would now go inside. It took me about twenty-five seconds to express my opinion of him and his conduct, and of the disgrace he was to the British

Empire, after which I left him standing where he was, and joined my friends, refusing to enter the prison in his company.

I repeat that this is an extreme case; but it illustrates, as I had only too much occasion to see, the way in which the educated Indian is treated by a large section of Anglo-Indians, who believe they are thus keeping the Indian in his proper place and teaching him respect for British rule.

THE SWADESHI MOVEMENT.

THAT evening we sailed down the river in a flat punt to the port of landing, and found we had some hours to wait for our steamer.

I spent the night in smoking and mosquito hunting in a wharf shed. Most of the next day we were sailing up the Brahmaputra river, and finally reached Mymensingh, where I was the guest of His Highness the Maharajah, occupying the same suite of rooms that had been used by Lord Curzon on the occasion of an official visit a few years previously. The village looked like a place in a state of siege. Every twenty yards or so two armed constables were posted, whilst the ordinary policemen were also a good deal in evidence. These armed and other police had been imported from a distance to preserve order in the village. The amusing thing was that as darkness set in, these guardians of law and order were marched off to the barracks, quite a mile and half from the town. They were kept standing on the roads in the hot sun all through the broad light of day; but when darkness came on, and when the vile revolutionaries whom they were there to suppress would—so one would think, at least—find an opportunity for committing their desperate deeds, the guardians of law and order were marched off to the security of their barracks. These special men are called the punitive force, and are quartered on villages, which are saddled with the cost, as a punishment for some offence, real or imaginary, against the majesty of the law.

Here I had another illustration of the way in which the dignity of Great Britain is upheld by those who represent her in this far-off land.

The Lieutenant-Governor was about to visit Mymensingh, and a committee was formed to prepare a reception. On that committee, by special invitation, were two agents of a local landowner of some considerable standing. Some time prior to this, there had been some petty disturbance in the village, and the house of this local landowner had the sides torn out by the police, who entered, without any warrant, under pretence of searching for arms and incriminating documents. I was supplied with photographs of the scene. The landowner, who himself resides at Calcutta, entered a suit for damages against the authorities, for the wanton destruction of his property, and this suit was still pending when the Governor paid his visit. The landowner, or, as they are called, the zemindar, had been asked to subscribe towards the fund for suitably receiving the Governor, and had subscribed Rs. 150, whereupon he received a card of invitation to attend the function of the Governor's reception. A few days before the reception, however, he was informed by a local official that unless he withdrew his action against the authorities for damage done to his property, the invitation would be withdrawn.

He appealed to the Governor, but all in vain; and in the end was not allowed to attend the reception. The case for damages was finally decided in his favour. Thus for refusing to assent to an illegal outrage, involving the destruction of property, this local gentleman was branded as a rebel not only by the local officials, but also by the Lieutenant-Governor himself. Such a thing would of course be impossible at home, though in India it was done apparently as a matter of course. Mymensingh is one of the proclaimed districts in which no meetings are permitted, and the police, armed and unarmed, were, as already stated, in evidence all day long.

From Mymensingh the next stage in the journey was Barisal, which we reached in the evening, and where apparently the entire population had turned out to offer their welcome. The way to the Dak bungalow was brilliantly illuminated, and the streets were filled with cheering crowds. I addressed a few words of thanks from the bungalow steps.

Among the information received at Barisal was the fact, subsequently substantiated by personal investigation, that in one part of the district, where, owing to the strength of the Swadeshi movement, nobody could be got to sell foreign goods, two policemen, who were still in the pay of the authorities, had been set up as shopkeepers. There were also further tales of houses being ransacked and pillaged by policemen without warrant or authority, and it was here I made the remark to a press interviewer that these things, together with the facts brought to my notice at Mymensingh, savoured more of Russian than of British methods, an opinion to which I adhere. Here also I had further particulars supplied me of the forcible abduction and violation of Hindu women by Mohammedan rowdies, and it was this I likened to Armenian atrocities.

I may here explain the meaning of Swadeshi. All over East Bengal, and, in fact, over the greater part of India, there has recently been a great development of this movement. It takes the form, in extreme cases, of boycotting foreign goods, and is intended to support and develop local industries. Lord Roberts, Lord Curzon, and practically everyone who has ever been identified with India, have preached the need for Swadeshi, though not, of course, boycott, and no one can visit the country, even for a brief period, without realising that the poverty-stricken condition of these hundreds of millions of patient, toiling peasants and weavers can never be even temporarily relieved until native industry has been developed. Owing to the feeling excited over the partition of Bengal, the Swadeshi movement is particularly strong in that province, where the inhabitants have taken a solemn vow not to purchase British goods until the partition has been repealed, and to do all they can to induce others to follow their example. They hope by this means so to injure British trade as to force the attention of the authorities at home to their grievances, and thus ensure their redress. The hope may be a vain one, but there it is.

In the main, this boycott has been conducted on strictly constitutional lines, although it well may be that here and there an instance may be found of the boundary of prudence having been overstepped, especially by zealous youths. Be this as it may, the fact remains that Swadeshi has a strong hold in the district, and in some of the villages no Bilati (foreign) goods are sold.

The case above referred to of a village where policemen had been set up as shopkeepers for the sale of foreign goods, is one of these. The Barisal magistrate denied all knowledge of the police being employed as shopkeepers. But on my way down the river, after leaving Barisal, the steamer stopped at the village in the early morning; I went ashore, not a very dignified figure, I fear, in a Japanese Kimono and with sandalled feet, and visited the shop, and found the facts to be substantially as set out above.

The land on which the shop stands is public land, and the lease is held by two local constables, who are still on duty. The shop, however, is nominally kept by the uncle-at-law of one of the two.

Here, again, I ask what would be thought at home if policemen were allowed to act in this manner? I question whether even in Ireland, of which India constantly reminded me, an instance of the public authorities acting in this fashion could be found? I may add that my first information of the case came from a Mohammedan shopkeeper from the village, who came to Barisal to see me, and who on bended knee implored me not to allow his business to be ruined by the police authorities. The point of this is that the action of the authorities in trying to suppress the Swadeshi movement is alleged to be taken in the interests of the Mohammedans.

But to return to Barisal. In the early days of Swadeshi a number of local gentlemen issued a signed printed document, in which they explained their reasons for being Swadeshists. The magistrate took exception to a portion of the circular, whereupon it was withdrawn, upon which the local police-superintendent issued a public statement, declaring that the men who had signed the memorial had admitted themselves to be guilty of sedition, and warning the public against them.

One gentleman of good social position, Aswini Kumar Dutt, who was thus charged, since deported without trial, who, like his father before him, has devoted his life and his fortune to educating the people, in the teeth of the petty opposition of the Government, though this is a recent development, raised an action for damages against the police-superintendent, and was awarded by the Courts Rs. 100/-. According to my information, not only were the legal expenses of the police officer, but also the damages awarded against him, paid from public funds, and he, instead of being reprimanded or dismissed, was promoted to a higher position in a neighbouring district.

AMONGST THE PEASANTS.

DACCA, our next stopping-place, is the new seat of Government for Eastern Bengal. Here I was informed, as I had been all the way along, that the reason for the special police and the precautionary measures generally was to protect the Mohammedans from being coerced by the Hindus into buying Swadeshi goods, which it was alleged were much higher in price than those which could be imported from abroad. One member of a Mohammedan deputation, who waited upon me at Dacca, repeated this statement, whereupon I sent out to a cloth merchant, who kept both kinds of goods, asking for samples of his goods, foreign and native, with prices. He sent across several bales, with the prices marked on, his manager accompanying them to receive the expected order, he not knowing what my object was. There I found by actual test, not only that the Swadeshi goods were of better quality, but also that for that particular class of goods, *dhotis*, the price was cheaper at Dacca than was the price of the foreign cloth.

I had a similar experience at Barisal, where I went up the river a few miles, and visited a couple of villages. The people turned out in large numbers when they heard that a visitor was in their midst. I made close inquiries as to whether they were wearing Swadeshi or Bilati cloth, and found that the majority were wearing, as they always had done, native goods, because they lasted longer and gave better value, and where they happened to wear Bilati it was only because it had been found more convenient to purchase that at the moment it was needed and not because of any preference for the foreign-made article.

The bulk of these villagers, be it remembered, are Mohammedans, and therefore the case of the authorities that they need protection against Hindu interference goes to the wall. Further, it has to be borne in mind that 75 per cent. of the people in East Bengal are Mohammedans, that the entire forces of the Government are behind them if they prefer foreign goods, and to speak of these fighting men thus situated as being intimidated by their Hindu neighbours into supporting Swadeshi is grotesque in its absurdity.

Moreover, there are tens of thousands of Mohammedan weavers who, prior to the introduction of the Swadeshi movement, were in a condition of chronic starvation for lack of employment, and who are now fully employed. It is not likely that these men are opposed to a movement which is finding them customers.

After leaving Dacca I had a most interesting experience. The steamer had occasion to stop for about an hour, and seeing a village near, I went ashore in company with some young students who had come many miles on the chance of seeing us as the steamer passed. On entering the village we came across a store—a building open on two sides and composed of bamboo poles and grass matting. A number of baskets containing grains and rice, gram, and a few other articles of general merchandise were set about on the floor, and in the midst of them sat the merchant himself, waiting for his customers to come. In a second small store opposite, I purchased some cigars, which were only found after much diligent search—a sure proof that they are not much in demand. Having essayed the smoking of one of them, I do not wonder at the demand being limited. I am pretty well seasoned to tobacco, but found this special brand of smoke more than a match for my powers.

From the store we strolled through the village till we came to the potters' huts. The Durga Puja, the great annual religious festival, was approaching, when an image is first carried about in a procession and afterwards thrown into the river. We found a potter at work making these images.

He and his family were well-built, handsome people, their hair nicely trimmed, oiled, and parted, and their skin of a beautiful mahogany colour. They belonged to the traditional potters' caste, and probably for hundreds, it may be for thousands, of years, they and their forbears have been potters. As a result they have inherited a wonderful skill, and the grace and beauty of the figures of the image, together with their anatomical accuracy, would have done credit to any sculptors in Europe. Many of those who do this work are unable to read, and have very little concern outside the affairs of their village; but the skill which enables them to do this marvellous work is the result of the accumulated experience of generations, transmitted from father to son, until it has become an instinct.

A naturalist, wishing to have some lizards modelled in clay, employed these men, and subsequently bore testimony to the fact that no flaw could be found in the work, every portion of the body being as perfectly reproduced as it appears in the living reptile.

I subsequently saw in Calcutta figures of men, women, and animals made by a similar class of workers, and can testify to their life-like appearance. Is the knowledge of anatomy, too, inherited, or whence comes it in men who know nothing of the teachings of school or college?

We saw the potter at work on his vessels also. A bamboo frame, covered with clay, is let into the ground, and this is the only wheel in the establishment.

After seeing these things, chairs were brought out and placed under the trees, cocoa-nuts were produced and cut open, and we drank the delicious milk fresh from the nut. Sweetmeats were also forthcoming, such sweetmeats as are to be had nowhere else in the world outside Bengal, and we feasted royally. A small crowd of villagers gathered round, the women keeping well out of sight in the background, and furtively eyeing us from a safe distance; everyone, young and old, quiet and dignified, though full of curiosity. A small money sum was offered, not by way of payment, but in recognition of what we had had, and it was refused with such dignity as to make me feel very small, and was only reluctantly taken at last on the understanding that it was to be spent by the children at the approaching festival. A magistrate in another part of India afterwards told me that they have the greatest possible difficulty in getting certain classes of the people to accept famine relief even when they are dying by inches of starvation. These, be it remembered, are the ryots—the peasants of India. Would that we had more of this feeling of self-respect elsewhere!

At Khulna, where unfortunately, I was unable to stay, the district magistrate, who is a Mohammedan, the superintendent of police, and practically the whole village turned out to receive us, and from Khulna we travelled back by night train to Calcutta.

This journey into the wilds, away from the beaten track, where tourists are seldom seen, and where there are no picture postcards, brought me into direct touch and contact with all classes and conditions of people in the disturbed area. Here was, so I had been told, the home of sedition, and some of the men whom I met were its high priests. The day may come, though I hope not, when the authorities in India may have to deal with sedition, and should it come, viceroys and subordinate officials will learn how cruelly they have been maligning men and women whose loyalty is beyond question, and whose only offence is love of country and a great consuming zeal to serve the Motherland, and make her prosperous as a contented part of the British Empire.

THE PARTITION OF BENGAL.

It may be convenient at this stage to explain somewhat in detail what is meant by the partition of Bengal.

During Lord Curzon's reign, the Province of Bengal was divided into two parts, each of which was given a Lieutenant-Governor and a Council, the new eastern province consisting of Assam and the eastern district of Bengal. The only official justification for the act that I have seen was that better administration was secured by the partition, though it is more than doubtful whether even this is the case. In the new eastern province of Bengal two-thirds of the population is Mohammedan, and many of the Mussulman leaders, therefore, support the partition, since it gives them a sphere within which their influence is dominant. There is, however, a strong body of educated Mohammedan opinion strongly opposed to the change.

For a number of years prior to the partition a feeling of unrest had been growing in Bengal. The Bengalee Hindu had, for three generations, taken full advantage of such education as the Government had offered, and had supplemented this by the erection of private primary and higher-grade schools. It is universally admitted, by friend and opponent alike, that the Hindu capacity for learning is scarcely equalled in any part of the world. Here is Sir Thomas Munro's testimony, after thirty years' experience: "They (the Hindus) are better accountants than Europeans, more patient and laborious, . . . and are altogether more efficient men of business." It is fashionable nowadays to sneer at the Hindu "Babu," but this testimony still holds good, as the many thousands of these men holding positions of trust and responsibility in Government offices, railway departments, banks, and business offices amply testifies. As a consequence of all this, there has arisen in Bengal an educated middle class, mainly Hindu, which, as might have been foreseen, frets against the barriers which the system of governing India erects around them in every direction, and interferes with their finding a healthy outlet for their energies. The system of education which has been pursued is now held responsible for the creation of so many educated men for whom the law offers almost the only outlet; but the Babu did not create the system, and cannot be held responsible for its results. It is altogether to his credit that he took full advantage of what was offered him, though even this is sometimes used as an argument to his discredit.

One of the theories of government in India is that before any great change is undertaken local opinion shall be consulted and, as far as possible, the wishes of localities shall be met before the change is effected—in its final form, at least. In the partition of Bengal, however, nothing of this kind took place. There are in Bengal men of title, social standing, and position—men, for example, like the late Maharajah of Mymensingh, who played the part of host to Lord Curzon when he visited the province. Improbable as it may seem, it is none the less true that the opinion of even such men was never invited, nor were they in any way consulted, regarding the partition. Not only so, but all local opinion, official and other, was bitterly hostile to Lord Curzon's proposals. When, therefore, the decree was issued disrupting the ancient kingdom of Bengal there was naturally much resentment, which found vent in public meetings, at which Lord Curzon and his policy were vigorously criticised.

At first it was expected that the British Parliament would have intervened to prevent the opinions of the educated classes in Bengal being flouted and outraged, as they were by Lord Curzon and his advisers; but when it was seen that this hope, like so many others in India, was a vain one, resort was had to other methods of calling attention to the question. For some years past Swadeshi had been in the air, meaning thereby the development of native industries to supply the Indian market. Just before the partition of Bengal took place this vague idea was seized upon, and it was formed into a positive creed, and a vigorous propaganda was carried on to induce the people to boycott all goods of British origin, and support home industries only. Bands of young men visited the markets and fairs, preaching Swadeshism, and appealing to merchants not to keep foreign goods. It was at first hoped by this method to make such an impression on British trade as to force the people at home to take some action in order that their industries might not be injured. Needless to say, this is a vain hope; but the Swadeshi movement has none the less come to stay. Many years must elapse before it can have any serious effect on imports, but meanwhile Indian industries are being developed, Hindu technical schools and colleges are being opened, and a healthy public, patriotic spirit is being evoked.

During this period of agitation the authorities were not idle. The Lieutenant-Governor of Eastern Bengal, Sir Bampfylde Fuller, resigned his position shortly after the partition in consequence of a difference of opinion between himself and the Viceroy, and Sir Launcelot Hare was appointed in his stead. I did not meet Sir Launcelot Hare during my visit, he being at a hill station, but all accounts I could gather indicated that he lacked that firmness and breadth of view so necessary in a man called upon to handle a somewhat delicate situation. When Sir John Hewett, the Lieutenant-Governor of the United Provinces, found trouble brewing in his province, he took prompt action to ascertain the cause, and, as far as possible, to meet the wishes of the people under his charge; and as a consequence the right of public meeting was never in any way curtailed in the province under his rule. In Eastern Bengal, however, other methods prevailed. The police were encouraged to bring charges based upon the most trivial incidents, and sometimes sheer concoctions, against individuals who were ardent Swadeshists. Some of those who were thus persecuted and prosecuted were amongst the finest men I met during my visit. When it was found that the people were not to be intimidated into abandoning their agitation against the partition, fresh measures were evoked. Punitive police were called in and quartered on the villages, entailing a heavy charge on the rates, and, finally, an ordinance was issued prohibiting all public meetings. The excuse for this ordinance was that the meetings were of a seditious character. Everything in India is seditious which does not slavishly applaud every act of the Government. An agitation to protest against the partition of Bengal and secure the repeal of the enactment is no more seditious in India than is, say, the Irish Home Rule movement at home. But the authorities in India will brook no public spirit, and at the time of my visit Eastern Bengal resembled more a country in a state of siege than a province under the British Crown in times of peace. Educational institutions were being interfered with, the theory of the authorities being that the schools were seed plots in which to develop seditious agitators. Because young men sympathised with the agitation, as they were bound to do, that was held to be proof of their disloyalty, and all sorts of irritating punitive steps were taken against them. As I have shown, not only did the police unduly interfere in the interests of those merchants who sold foreign goods, but, when necessary, they themselves were, in at least one case, encouraged to open stores for the sale of such goods.

At the end of six months the ordinance prohibiting public meetings expired, but the Government of India meanwhile had rushed through a new law giving them power to enact a similar, and even more stringent, prohibition at will, and under its provisions Eastern Bengal was at once declared a proclaimed area, and so the educated and enlightened portion of the people in Eastern Bengal—the most enlightened and educated people in India—are gagged and bound, and are practically at the mercy of the police. The new law enacts that if twenty people assemble without the authorisation of the police, even if it be at a funeral or marriage, or at any social function, or in connection with a religious ceremony, the police may charge them with holding a seditious meeting, and upon those responsible for the gathering and those attending it will rest the burden of disproof. Only those who have seen on the spot the workings of Eastern police methods can realise what this means. If the intention of the Government is to make people disloyal and to give them good cause for being seditious, then, indeed, they are following the right course in Eastern Bengal.

In addition to the political difficulties of the

question there are the religious. Some Mohammedans, for the reasons stated above, naturally favour partition, and believing the authorities to be on their side, the more rowdy element among them in some well-authenticated instances, at least, took full advantage of the opportunity thus given. One case which went to the High Court will give an instance of how justice is administered in this portion of the province. On the occasion of the visit to Comilla of the Nawab of Dacca there was a Mohammedan procession. The Nawab Salimullah was the leading Mohammedan in Eastern Bengal. Some years ago he inherited a huge fortune, but succeeded in running through it and got so hopelessly into debt that he had to declare himself unfit to manage his own estates, and to place himself under the jurisdiction of the Court of Wards.

Prior to the Nawab's visit, outrages on Hindu women by Mohammedan rowdies had been numerous, and a rumour had got abroad that the procession intended to attack a Hindu quarter for the purpose of ravishing and carrying off the women. As the procession neared this quarter two shots were fired, one of which killed a poor unfortunate man. A Hindu gentleman was apprehended on the charge of having fired one of the shots, and the case came before the District Magistrate, Mr. Cummings, who found the man guilty. He admitted that there was no proof to show that the accused had fired the shot which killed the victim, and the High Court subsequently could find no proof to show that the man had fired any shot at all.

But Mr. Cummings argued that two shots had been fired, one of which killed a man, and though it would probably never be known who had fired the fatal shot, he felt it his duty to condemn the person before him to death. When the case came before the High Court of Appeal the judges ridiculed Mr. Cummings's methods in probably the most scathing indictment ever indulged in by a court of justice. They showed that important official witnesses who had offered themselves as evidence were not allowed to testify, the presumption being that they would have been on the side of the accused, and in the end they upheld the appeal and set the condemned man at liberty.

I give this as typical of the way in which justice is administered by many of the officials in the disturbed districts in Eastern Bengal. I declare in the most emphatic manner that at the time of my visit *there was no sedition in Eastern Bengal;* there was resentment, deep and bitter, against the partition; there was a longing patriotic desire to have the partition order revoked, or at least modified in such a way as would restore Bengal to its former unity. The way in which the Government met this perfectly legitimate agitation and demand was to declare all identified with it as seditious rebels, and treat them as so many outlaws. In the end this can have only one result. The Hindu is by nature loyal, patient, and long-suffering; but there are limits even to Hindu endurance, and those limits have probably been reached in the eastern districts of Bengal. The Swadeshi movement grows and spreads on every hand. Where the Government interferes with private schools, which receive a Government grant, these are cut off, sometimes voluntarily, from the receipt of all Government aid, and are then carried on as purely voluntary agencies. Hindu colleges on similar lines, including the Technical College in Calcutta, are being staffed by trained teachers, who have given up valuable and lucrative appointments to serve their people. Schools and colleges for women are being opened, and altogether the misguided action of Lord Curzon and his advisers is having the effect of stimulating the Hindu people into a degree of energetic activity hitherto unknown and deemed to be all but impossible.

The partition of Bengal was a huge blunder; the method adopted of bringing it about a greater blunder still. Those who think the agitation against the partition is confined to the Babu class little know the facts of the case. I had opportunities of meeting in private consultation with members of the titled aristocracy, the landed gentry, of the Legislative Council, judges and leading lawyers, and although most of these were strong in their condemnation of the agitation and the methods connected with it, they were no less strong in their feeling that partition was a great mistake which ought to be rectified at the earliest possible moment. One method by which the blunder might be retrieved would be the adoption of the plan proposed by Lord MacDonnell: the transference from Western to Eastern Bengal of two revenue divisions—Burdwan and the Presidency division, with Calcutta—and the raising of the enlarged Province to the status of a Council Government, on the model of Madras and Bombay, with a Governor appointed from England. This would have the effect of reuniting the Bengali-speaking people under one administration, and would at the same time provide Bengal with a Government in accordance with modern needs. Lord Morley missed a great opportunity when on taking office he did not repeal the partition ordinance and reconsider the whole question *de novo*. Even now it is not too late to re-open the question and restore peace to the province and remove a rankling feeling of injustice from the heart and mind of the Hindu people. In the archives of the Indian Office is a scheme of partition which the Bengal Civil Service prepared and the Hindus were willing to accept. It met the difficulty of administering so large an area from one centre, yet left the ancient landmarks untouched.

BENARES.

Benares is the holy city of Hinduism. What Jerusalem is to the Hebrew, and Mecca to the Moslem, that is Benares to the Hindu. It is built on the high north bank of the Ganges, and broad flights of steps lead right down into the water. Great temples of various Hindu sects, and one Mohammedan mosque, front the river, their foundations deep down beneath the surface of the water, and their walls of solid masonry rising high up into the air. At one place a temple has subsided, until only the upper parts are to be seen. Some of the buildings are very old, whilst others are quite modern, nearly every one being the gift of some rich Maharajah or merchant.

Every day hundreds of pilgrims come from all parts of India to Benares to bathe in the Ganges and worship in the temples, and on special occasions the pilgrims are reckoned by the thousand. In the narrow, tortuous lanes learned pundits, religious devotees, fakirs, ascetics, and ordinary beggars are seated in long rows, or move about, bowl in hand, soliciting arms. A few grains of rice seemed the most common form of gift. The hair of some of the holy men, matted and tatted, reaches almost to the ground, whilst others again have it coiled in plaits round the head. In some cases I estimated that the coils, if unwound, would measure twelve or fifteen feet in length. There are charitable agencies which feed these ascetics. The temples were crowded. In the Cow Temple some sacred cattle moved about among the worshippers. Shrines are common, and I noticed that at the entrance to one temple there was a small image in the arch of the doorway, and each worshipper, in passing, either sprinkled water from the Ganges or flung a handful of flowers at it before entering.

Fascinating as are the lanes and bazaars of the city, it is the river front which is the chief attraction. About four in the morning men, women, and children begin to crowd down the steps towards the water's edge. After thoroughly washing themselves, standing up to the waist in the water, they take off and wash also the garment in which they have bathed. Many of them also bring their brass household utensils, which they wash and scour till the bright metal shines again in the sunlight. There is one ghat (bathing-place) reserved for women, but mixed family bathing is the rule. The idea is purification, not merely of the body, but of the soul. The water of the Ganges is holy, and though it does not look any more inviting than does the Thames at Westminster or the Clyde at the Broomielaw, still, being holy, neither sewage nor dead bodies can pollute it. The Burning Ghat is a gruesome sight. The Hindus cremate their dead, and it is done in the open air. On the occasion of my second visit to the ghat, five bodies were being burned. A pile of wood, which varies in size according to the wealth or poverty of the family, is built, and on this the body is laid and the pile set ablaze. The relatives sit a little distance apart, bare-footed, their bowed heads covered with mantles, while one member of the family attends to the fire. When the body has been reduced to ashes, water from the Ganges is thrown on the smouldering embers, which are then thrown into the river. In East Bengal I found that crematoriums were becoming common; but here in Benares there is no such innovation.

Mr. Moti Chand, a leading gentleman of the city, placed his finely-appointed houseboat at my disposal, and on this, accompanied by a number of local gentlemen, I spent an hour on the river in the gloaming. Next morning, Supt. Murray sent a police-boat, on which I had a second outing, up and down the river front. The scene to Western eyes was wondrously attractive. The glorious sun, the majestic buildings, the weird, sad music and clang of bells from the temples, and the monotonous chants of the devotees; the minarets, towers, and domes, some plated with gold, others of brown and white stone; the varied architecture, from the ancient Jain to the modern Hindu; the moving myriads of brown figures clad in bright-coloured, loose-flowing garments, the women laden with ornaments, rings hanging from the ears and the nose, with bangles innumerable encircling arms and ankles, and rings on fingers and toes—these, with the beggars and devotees, made up a medley of sights and sounds which photographed itself on the memory in a way never to be erased.

Benares is famous for its silks and brass work. The more common and useful kinds of silks received some impetus from the Swadeshi movement, and the Government were, so I was informed, about to open, or cause to be opened, a silk factory, in which a modern loom and the jacquard frame would be introduced. At present the looms, like those of the muslin weavers of Dacca, are of the most primitive kind, and the wages of the weavers range from one to four annas a day—that is, from one penny to fourpence. Swadeshi is also helping the brassworkers, and German goods are not so much in vogue as formerly. This is well. There are, however, higher branches of these industries which are not so fortunate. In one of the narrowest of the lanes, in a dingy building, is the shop-factory of Messrs. Bhagwan D. Gopi Nath, a firm which has been in business for hundreds of years, and produces brocaded silk worked in gold and silver wire, the Oriental grandeur of which must be seen to be believed. In days gone past the great princes and rulers, Nawabs, and Maharajahs of India, were supplied by this firm. Now the old native pride is dying, and the coffers of many of the petty chiefs and rulers are so depleted that there is no longer much demand. And so the industry is decaying. The late Lady Curzon was a faithful patron of the firm, and Queen Alexandra has also been a purchaser; but these are isolated cases, and unless something be done speedily workmen, who have thousands of years of inherited skill and artistic feeling in their nimble fingers, will go the way of so many Indian crafts, and become extinct.

There had been no "sedition" at Benares, nor anywhere else throughout the United Provinces. Agitation there had been, as everywhere, for reform, but owing to the excellent relations existing between the officials, from the Lieutenant-Governor downwards, there had been no occasion for coercive or repressive measures. A touch of human sympathy goes a long way in India—pity that it should be so rare. There is a very fine library in Benares, founded in 1872 by an Indian gentleman, Sinkata Prasad, and named the Carmichael Library, after the then Chief Commissioner. It has thousands of volumes, and a reading-room well supplied with newspapers and magazines. In the large room of the library I met the leading residents of the place, and received their good wishes. Among those who took part was Mr. Mallik, who contested St. George's Hanover Square, in the Liberal interest at the last General Election.

Benares is, I believe, the headquarters of the famous nautch dancers, who are said to command fabulous prices sometimes for their performances, but these I did not see. In the evening, however, a young conjurer came to the hotel and performed on the verandah in the open air such wonders as stupefied the bewildered onlookers. He made a mango tree grow from a seed in a pot in about half an hour, but I thought this the least wonderful and most clumsy part of the performance. He had no curtains, tables, or other accessories of any kind, and I sat with my feet on the rug on which he squatted, and betimes had the feeling that I must be bewitched, so mysterious were some of the things he did. For an hour's entertainment he netted the sum of 3s. 8d., of which a party of four Americans travelling round the world contributed 6d. each! Next morning, and within fifty feet of the room in which I slept, a man and a snake were found dead side by side. It is thought the snake bit the man, who thereupon killed it, and subsequently died of the bite. I have a photograph of the two dead bodies. The man's little son, aged nine, had slept peacefully all through the night unaware of the tragedy which was being enacted.

A LAND OF HUNGER.

ELEVEN miles from Benares is the village of Chaybopore. I selected that for a visit because it has a school and a police-station, and is therefore a place of some importance. Being close to Benares, I assumed that it would show more prosperity than those villages further removed from a big centre of population. Chaybopore may be taken as fairly typical of the many villages which I visited.

The school was visited first. It consisted of a thatch roof, supported on bamboo poles. There were 250 boys in attendance, the fees ranging from one pice (¼d.) a month for infants, to 4d. for the more advanced classes. The boys were mostly the sons of ryots. There was also a pupil training class, with five students. A girls' school had lately been opened in a dingy mud hut, given free by its owner, who was also the teacher. His salary is five rupees (6s. 8d.) *a month.* Sitting round the wall on the floor were the girls, most of them very young, for at thirteen they must leave *to be married.* It is considered a disgrace to have an unmarried daughter over fourteen years of age. Some of them had trinkets on, the nose-drop being common; but many of them were in rags, and most of them half starved. Bright, active little things they proved to be, as with a bamboo pen dipped in whiting, they traced out the alphabet on their black wooden "slates." For a great wonder no fees were charged in the girls' school. The entire school is under the control of the District Board, and when the fees fall short of the outlay that body makes good the deficit.

The children come from a distance of two miles round, and the parents show a laudable desire to give them such education as the school provides. Children coming from a distance bring their food with them. I opened half a dozen of the little food parcels to see what they contained. In one, which contained a day's food supply for four growing boys, there were a few ounces of uncooked maize—that, and nothing more. Others had split peas, and others, again, a like weight of Marna, which is a kind of hemp seed, about the size of a pin-head. That is to say, that each of these growing lads, whose ages ranged from eight to twelve years, subsist on bird seed, and get less of that each day than an amateur bird fancier at home would give to a pet canary.

The salary of the headmaster is twenty-five rupees (33s. 4d.) per month; his assistants receiving from ten to fifteen rupees. No English is taught or spoken. For bright, active boys fit to take a higher education at a secondary school in Benares there are free scholarships; not too many of these, however, the total number for the entire province, comprising thousands of villages, with a population of 40,000,000, being only forty-three scholarships! The figures speak for themselves. At the corner of many houses little crescent-shaped cakes were drying in the sun. These were made of cow-dung, which, after being dried, is carried into Benares to be *sold as fuel*. The cooking in the village is mostly done by dried grass and leaves.

From the school we went into the centre of the village, the dominie and his staff leading. Imagine a collection of mud huts, with some of matted palm leaves, all thrown higgledy-piggledy together, with goats and cattle moving about or being fed from earthenware troughs, and you have the village. I noticed that in the older huts the lintels and doorposts were carved. At the village store I saw the pulses and grains which compose the food of the people, and learned from the store-keeper that rice was selling at six seers per rupee, whereas formerly one rupee bought fifteen seers. Wheat had advanced similarly. That is to say, the price of food has practically trebled in, say, ten years.

At first the villagers held aloof, thinking that I was an English doctor who had come to vaccinate them. But at length they were induced to come together, and we were soon on quite good terms with each other. They brought out for my inspection handfuls of boiled rice, which was being prepared for their one and only meal, and pieces of bread, some made thick like Scotch oatmeal bannocks, and others thin, like ordinary oatmeal cake. It was quite black, and made from the Marna seed spoken of above. I went inside their hovels, and saw how they lived. One poor woman, her face averted and partially covered by a scarf, showed me her bed. It was the ragged remains of a thick cotton sheet, which at night was put on the ground, without bedding or bedclothes of any other kind. The previous year had seen a partial failure of the crop, and, owing to the drought, there had been no sowing done for what should have been the approaching harvest, and so they were already face to face with famine. They had already, owing to the partial failure of the crop, sold their jewellery and mortgaged their land to pay their rent and buy food, and so were quite destitute of all resources. I had been cross-examining one old man as to how he lived, and finally said to him: "Last year you mortgaged your land to pay your rent and buy food; this year you have no land to mortgage, and famine is coming. What will you do this year?" Every rib could be seen through his skin, and his face was gaunt and drawn, but his faith was strong. Looking me in the face, he answered simply, "Trust in God." This man is a heathen. "Why not trust in the Government?" I asked. That, however, had not entered into his thoughts.

I want it to be understood that the people whose case I am now dealing with are the *farming* class, the ryots—men whose forbears for generations have been occupiers and tillers of the soil. Beneath these is the coolie, or labouring class, who have no land, and who hire themselves out for wages. The men I met and conversed with were shrewd, kindly, and sensible, and very intelligent. They were paying for the education of their children at the expense of their stomach. The old dominie and his staff have a zeal for education, and when a parent is unable to pay the school fees, as sometimes happens, they will pay them out of their own scanty salaries.

If it be urged that I saw them at their worst, owing to the failure of last year's crop, then the reply is that it is only a question of degree, that in normal times they are starved, and that when scarcity comes they have no resources to fall back upon. Their normal condition is one of indebtedness, since before they can clear off the debt of one bad season another is upon them. Their honesty is proverbial. They borrow and lend on word of mouth, and the repudiation of a debt is almost unknown. They are strict teetotalers and vegetarians, and if they still cling to primitive methods of cultivation, that is mainly because they know no better, and because they are bereft of heart or hope. That they have seen better days brooks no denial. Their customs, their raiment, the way in which the women who can afford it adorn themselves with jewellery, the carved woodwork on the doors and lintels of their houses, their innate courtesy and gentleness—all these tell of a condition of things vastly different from what we see to-day; and, as we shall see later, it scarce admits of a doubt that their position has worsened considerably under British rule.

After a brief visit to the police-station I was motored back to Benares. Here, as elsewhere, I learned that the salaried, or, as we should say at home, the lower middle-class, are in much the same condition as the ryots. The cost of living has more than doubled, the wages of coolies have gone up, but the salaries of clerks and petty officials have remaïned almost stationary. They, too, are starving, and, like the poor clerk at home, they must keep up appearances. Their case was being considered by the authorities, and special famine measures for their relief have since been taken. What they stand most in need of is a permanent increase of salary corresponding in some degree to the increase in the price of food.

SEDITION IN THE NORTH.

From Benares I visited in turn Agra, Lucknow, Cawnpore, Delhi, and Lahore. Each and all of these is a centre of special interest, and with the aid of Murray's Handbook I could write many entertaining articles on what I saw. But time and space forbid.

The building which impressed me most was the Taj at Agra, which more than justifies the description of a "poem in marble." If one could imagine the divine afflatus of Shelley or Keats transformed into carved marble, that would be the Taj. It was erected by a Mohammedan ruler, Shah Jahan, to commemorate his wife. As it stands it is only part completed, the original design having included a similar building on the other side of the river, with a marble bridge connecting the two.

At Lucknow the great Mohammedan Mosque, seen, as I saw it, in the pale light of a young crescent moon, impressed the imagination with a reverential awe. Outside royal Delhi stands the Kutab Minar, a great tower, rising two hundred and fifty feet skywards, and surrounded by an ancient Hindu temple with wonderful carved marble pillars. The latter were defaced by the Mohammedans, who in some cases contented themselves with chipping away the features of the Hindu deities, whilst in others they transformed them into floral decorations. Here also stands an iron pillar, the origin of which is a mystery. Its age has been variously estimated at from one thousand to fifteen hundred years. Nowadays, its production would be a mere commonplace item; but even a hundred years ago it would have constituted a marvel in the way of production. It is a standing proof that the metallurgic arts had attained to a high degree of development in India many centuries ago. Delhi, more than any other part of India perhaps, is a microcosm of the past. Two thousand five hundred years ago—that is, five hundred years before the birth of Christ, and half a thousand years before the Roman invasion brought the first gleams of civilisation to Western Europe—art, science, learning, and religion flourished in the ancient Hindu kingdom of which Delhi was the capital. But I must not dwell on these things, or I shall be led too far afield.

The further north one travels in India, the more is the soldier in evidence. Even from the railway carriage the military cantonment is the most common object which meets the eye. The fear of a Russian invasion is responsible for the fact that all up through the north and the north-west the military authorities have had pretty much their own way. Millions have been expended in the erection of cantonments and fortifications, and millions more are being squandered in their maintenance and upkeep. I am no military man, and therefore my opinion may not be worth much in matters of this kind, but others competent to form an opinion hold strongly that most of this is so much money wasted. Whatever may have been the danger in the past, now that a friendly Afghanistan stands as a barrier between Moscow and Delhi, and since we are at peace with Russia, surely the crushing burden of militarism under which India groans might be sensibly relieved.

Delhi and the surrounding district were alleged to be storm centres of the seditious movement, and many were the gruesome tales of treasonable plots and risings which were dished up in the columns of the *Times*. That there was some unrest is certain, and a brief examination of the causes will enable readers to form a fair estimate of the reliance to be placed upon press estimates of what constitutes sedition in India.

Several main causes contributed to the unrest. The growth of an educated middle-class, the deepening and growing poverty of the ryots, the prevalence with monotonous continuance of plague and famine, the irksome restrictions imposed by Government, and the growing alienation between East and West, all had their share in producing the discontent which journalists and officials classed as sedition. But more than all these put together was the growth of the military spirit, which is yearly becoming an increasing factor in the administration of Indian affairs. Freedom and militarism are mutually antagonistic forces, and where the former flourishes the latter cannot thrive. Not only is this the case, but the military forces, neither knowing nor understanding the spirit of civil freedom, take alarm at the slightest display thereof.

This fact was curiously brought to light in Delhi during April and May of the year 1907. As a matter of fact, there can be no doubt that the military developed a state of "blue funk" as the jubilee of the Great Mutiny approached. Plague was raging within the city and as many as two hundred and fifty funerals were to be seen passing through the streets in one day. For the province of which Delhi forms the chief city the deaths from plague were for a period *seventy-five thousand per week.*

Whilst the plague was thus raging and fear was in the minds of the people, the municipal authorities of Delhi saw fit, for some reason or another, to double the municipal assessment, which led to a strong agitation by way of protest, during which public meetings were held and memorials were sent to the authorities. This was in April; and as May 10th was the fiftieth anniversary of the outbreak of the Mutiny, prejudiced newspaper correspondents and easily-imposed-upon military officers coupled the agitation with the jubilee, and came to the conclusion that a second rising was impending.

One of the best of the civil officials that I met in India gave me this warning: "Always," he said, "make allowance for the fact when listening to statements from peasants that the native mind is so constituted as to know intuitively what you want to be told, and to make his statement fit in with your wishes." If this friendly hint was needed for a mere wayfarer like myself, how much more so was it in the case of police officials? But the military authorities ignored it and thus it happened that alarming tales were freely poured into the credulous ears of Anglo-Indian journalists, who not only swallowed them greedily, but retailed them again with a truly Oriental wealth of imagination. As May 10th approached, the agitation against the municipal assessment in Delhi still continuing, the military authorities made up their minds for the worst. The gates of Delhi were strongly guarded by military patrols, and no Indian was allowed to pass out or in after dark. Guns and ammunition were put in special positions and trained on the city, ready for use at a moment's notice.

It so happened that at this same time a new tramway was being laid through the city, and on the evening of May 10th one of the contractors tried to cheat his workmen of a portion of their wages, whereupon they set upon him and gave him a good pommelling, which, doubtless, he richly deserved. A half-drunken Eurasian (who was subsequently placed under restraint) saw the fight, and rushed off, hot foot, to the European Club, and informed the panic-stricken inmates that Delhi had risen, that Europeans were being butchered, and that already the streets were drenched with English blood. The alarm spread from the club to the cantonment, and for twelve mortal hours a real reign of terror existed in the European quarters.

Fortunately for the city, the young magistrate who had charge of civil affairs kept his head, and prevented a development which might have led to the most disastrous results. Whilst Europeans were barricading their houses, patrolling their premises, shot-gun in hand, and preparing generally to sell their lives dearly, the native quarter of the city itself was going about its business and pleasure as usual, knowing nothing of all the terror which was being exhibited in the outside English quarters. Those who remember the blood-curdling reports which were cabled home at the time through Reuter's and other agencies about sedition and mutiny in Delhi will be astonished to learn that these had no other foundation than the drunken imagination of the dissolute character referred to above, coupled with the over-wrought mental condition of the military authorities. Nothing could better illustrate the aloofness of the military authorities from the people than the incident here set down.

When the municipal authorities saw that their proposed new assessment was being so hotly resented by the people, and was likely to lead to a passive resistance to all taxes on the part of the tradesmen and householders of the city, they withdrew their proposals, and the agitation at once subsided. It is on such slender foundations that the outcry about sedition and mutiny has been built up round Delhi. As the matter is of some importance, I will give one or two other illustrations from other centres, because it is of the first importance that the British people should understand the true facts of the situation as I saw them with my own eyes, and secured documentary and official evidence to prove, during my brief sojourn in India.

MORE ABOUT SEDITION IN THE NORTH.

One of the alleged hotbeds of sedition was Etawah in the United Provinces. Here, it was alleged, a seditious plot had been discovered by the police in which a number of Hindu officials were engaged in a plot to massacre the European settlement. Documentary evidence was produced in support of the charge, and the local magistrate actually prepared warrants for the deportation (without trial) of two of the leading conspirators. When the warrants were forwarded to the Governor for his signature, he, with that strong common-sense which has characterised his term of office, decided on having an independent inquiry before taking action, and sent down two of his most trusted officials to investigate the matter on the spot. These men visited Etawah, inquired into the circumstances, and were speedily convinced that the whole thing was a malicious police plot, and that the incriminating documents had been concocted and the signatures forged.

The result of the inquiry was to entirely exonerate the men who had been charged, and to fix the guilt on certain fellow-officials of theirs, who, in order to supply their superiors with the kind of sensation which they thought would please them, had concocted the whole blood-curdling tale. Warrants were issued for the arrest of those who had worked up this criminal conspiracy, but, strange to relate, no arrests were made. Here, however, is a case wherein but for the level-headedness of the Governor, a number of innocent men of good character and social position would have been deported, and further proof supplied to the gullible public at home of the existence of sedition in India. A little inquiry in other cases of "sedition" would, I am convinced, have had a similar ending.

For the purpose of this chapter I will take Lahore and Rawalpindi together, although they are many miles apart. The argricultural districts round about these places were undoubtedly in an agitated condition. Some years previously the Chenab irrigation canal had been made, which opened up a barren district, and led to its being colonised. Many of the colonists were ex-soldiers. The land, which had formerly been sandy waste, proved to be a veritable garden when irrigated by the canal waters. The settlers, however, found the conditions of their settlement very irksome. Restrictions and restraints abounded on every hand, and a colonist was not even allowed to visit his own family outside the colony without obtaining a special permit. Fines were the order of the day, and although I cannot charge my memory with the total sum thus exacted from the peasants in the course of a single year, still it was enormous. When at the back of all this the Government of the Punjab passed a new Act still further restricting the liberties of the colonists, and confiscating their property where they died without male issue, the colonists revolted, and an agitation ensued. At the same time a heavy increase was made in the irrigation water charges, although the canal was already returning 25 per cent. on the capital sunk in its construction. Whilst this was happening in the Chenab colony the rents (revenue) payable by the peasantry had been increased 25 per cent. in the Rawalpindi district under the new revenue settlement which had just been completed.

The Indian ryot is long-suffering and slow to anger, but these various vexatious imposts proved more than he could bear, and he commenced to agitate for some redress, and in this he was backed by the native Press of Delhi, Hindu and Mohammedan alike. It so happens that in this part of India *Begar* is common. *Begar* is a system which comes down from the days of native rule, when a chief, requiring men for any purpose, commandeered the number needed, and set them to work at their allotted task. Petty European officials, in the face of the prohibition of the Government, have tried to live up to this tradition, and many were the cases recited to me in which workmen and peasants were compelled, under threat of imprisonment, to leave their own work and to build a house or act as carriers for the servants of the British Raj. In one of these cases a British official had secured two men to accompany him on tour. Their clothing was of the scantiest; shelter there was none for them, and during the night one, or both men were frozen to death.

An Indian paper published in Lahore, the *Punjabi*, commenting on the case, called attention to the fact that even when Indians were murdered the punishment meted out to Europeans was very slight, and cited several instances in support of the statement. This was held to be rank sedition, and the editor and publisher were tried and convicted for this offence. On the day when they were being taken to prison after conviction a number of their fellow-townsmen, by whom they were known and respected, turned out to witness their removal. The day was wet; the horses employed to draw the carriage in which were the prisoners were of poor quality, and in consequence progress was slow. Meanwhile the crowd of sympathisers kept augmenting and cheering until the horses refused to go further, and the wretched cavalcade came to a standstill in the mud, whilst the prisoners were transferred from the carriage in which they were to one better equipped with horses.

Let it be noted that at this stage no attempt was made by the crowd to rescue the prisoners, which, in the mind of the authorities, was the object for which the crowd had gathered. During the course of the day some horse-play took place, which was called a riot, and for which ten men were arrested, of whom seven were convicted. An appeal was taken to the High Court, when four of the convicted men were liberated and three of the convictions upheld, although in one case the sentence was reduced. The High Court held that there had been no riot, but only a case of simple assault. Among others who had taken part in the agitation on behalf of the peasants was Lala Lajpat Rai, a local gentleman of spotless character, high aim, and self-sacrificing disposition. There was no crime which was not imputed to this man, even including intrigue with the Ameer of Cabul by the vitriolic Anglo-Indian Press.

When I received the Mohammedan deputation at Lahore, its spokesman, a gentleman occupying a good educational position in the town, went out of his way to assure me that while he was strongly opposed to Lala Lajpat Rai's methods of religious controversy, he still regarded him as a man of the highest character and noble aims, and that his deportation was a grave miscarriage of justice. It is alleged—with what degree of truth I know not—that Lord Kitchener threatened to resign unless an example was made of Lala Rajpat Rai. The authorities, however, had nothing against him, save that he was an agitator who voiced the grievance of the heavily-burdened peasants, and so, as he had broken no law and could not be convicted in any court of justice, the only thing left was to order his deportation without trial, which was accordingly done. He was sent to Burma, where he was kept a prisoner for six months. So much for sedition and riot in Lahore!

At Rawalpindi the peasants' agitation against the heavy increase in rent, 33 per cent., was very strong, and there, also, a number of educated Indian gentlemen were lending the weight of their influence to assist the ryots to obtain redress. The local magistrate, a hot-headed, tactless sort of man, thought he would like to try the effect of prosecution on some of his tormentors, and so he summoned them to meet him in the court-house on a certain day, to show cause why they should not be tried for sedition. This act of his would be ludicrous, but for what ensued. The Government, when notified of what he had done, refused to sanction his insane procedure, and ordered him to desist. He did not notify his intended victims of this fact, but on the appointed day proceeded to the court-house, where the gentlemen accused sent him a polite intimation that they refused to countenance his illegal procedure and did not intend to recognise his summons. The high-handed action of the magistrate had set both the town of Rawalpindi and the surrounding district in a ferment, and on the day on which the illegally-summoned champions of popular rights were to appear before the magistrate the peasants gathered in great force to stand by their friends. During the course of the day there were several cases of street broils, in which a mission station was set fire to, but no one was arrested. Ten or twelve days after these events fifty of the leading citizens of the town, including the gentlemen above referred to whom the magistrate had wanted to try for sedition, were suddenly seized by the police and cast into prison. These men, all of them of good social standing and position, educated, and leading lights in Rawalpindi society, applied for bail, which was refused, and for four and a half months they were kept in prison, awaiting trial.

Fortunately for them, the magistrate sent down by the Government to try the case was able to rise above local prejudice, and in the end he acquitted all the accused, characterised the evidence against them as having been fabricated, and frankly charged the prosecuting witnesses with perjury. The Viceroy, Lord Minto, on learning the effect which the Colonisation Bill above referred to was having upon the colonists and their relations in the army, promptly vetoed it, with the full concurrence of his Government. At the same time the proposal to increase the irrigation water charges was postponed for a year, and thereupon the entire "seditious" agitation subsided. The peasants had won, and naturally settled down into their wonted attitude of peaceful cultivation of the soil. The version of the authorities is that the deportation of Lala Lajpat Rai and the apprehension of the rebellious lawyers at Rawalpindi brought peace; whereas, as a matter of fact, peace came when the causes which had led to the agitation—to wit, the doubling of the municipal assessment at Delhi, the confiscatory canal colony legislation, and the increase of the already heavy water charges—were abandoned.

These, then, are the true facts of the "Sedition in the North" of which such distorted accounts appeared in the Press at the time, and which is still believed in by that section of Anglo-Indian society at home whose prejudice against everything affecting the life and happiness of the people of India is invulnerable. Part of the charges levelled against Lala Lajpat Rai and his co-patriots was that they were spreading sedition in the army. That the army was affected, is, I think, extremely probable, remembering that it is from this part of India that the army is chiefly recruited, and that those who were the victims of the Government's oppressive policy were the fathers, sons, and brothers of the men who compose the army. It was the Government of the Punjab, not the agitators, who were responsible for the unrest in the army. The Punjabi soldier, drawn from the peasant class to which he would one day again return, naturally sympathised with his own people in their day of trouble. Had the army been recruited to any extent from the districts of Eastern Bengal, the partition would have effected it in the same way, and would in all likelihood have been withdrawn, as were the Canal Colonisation Bill and the excessive water charges. The moral is obvious. The Government of India did not come to the rescue of the peasantry out of any sense of justice, but simply through the fear that if the injustice were persisted in dire results might accrue to the Indian Army.

HOW INDIA IS GOVERNED.

THE nominal capital of India is Calcutta, but for eight months in the year Simla is the seat of Government. The climate in Lower Bengal during September is of the worst possible description. The heat is great and the air moist, so that all one's wearing apparel is always clammy, and green fungi grows on one's boots and shoes. In the Punjab in October the air, as I experienced it, is dry and hot, with an occasional dust storm, which darkens the face of the earth and produces more physical discomfort than one cares to recall. Simla is a hill station seven thousand feet above the sea. The roads have been scalloped out of the mountain sides, and the houses seem to cling to the rocks like limpets. The heat is temperate, the air pure, and away in the distance can be seen the snow-clad heights of the Himalayas. It is to this haven of comfort that the Government of India flies for refuge from the scorching heat of the plains.

The political atmosphere of the place is as calm and serene as the natural. Away down in the sultry plains, seven thousand feet below, millions of human beings are steeped in never ending poverty, their loved ones perhaps dying like flies of plague and famine, and they themselves always hungry. To me it had appeared, when visiting the plague and famine stricken villages, as though a black cloud enveloped the lives of the people of the plains with never a gleam of sunlight athwart the gloom. But in Simla all was changed, as though by the stroke of a magician's wand. In its splendidly appointed offices, competent, capable men compile and prepare their reports out of the material supplied to them by their officials. In most countries something in the nature of a gulf separates the governors from the governed; but here the gulf becomes an unbridged chasm. The officials in the villages are face to face with the hard, grimy facts of the situation, but before their reports reach Simla they have undergone a process of sifting and purification, during which all the grosser elements have been precipitated and only rose-tinted ether reaches that serene height. Tons of blue books will there prove conclusively that the condition of the ryot is everything that the heart of man could desire if only wicked agitators would leave him alone.

The Government of India in its present form resembles a huge military despotism tempered somewhat by a civil bureaucracy. Every attempt to win even the smallest modicum of popular rights is regarded by the Olympians who inhabit the heights of Simla as a menace to the stability of the Empire. The men in charge of affairs are broad-minded, enlightened, competent, and capable in most of the affairs of life, but concerning India and its Government they for the most part have but one idea—to maintain things as they are. Personally, they are not to blame. They are the inheritors of a system of government which has crystallised with the process of the years, and which binds them as much as it does the poor, hapless ryot. Change means trouble, and there is no free air of public criticism to force it on them or to leaven with its influence the harshness of the official régime. Everything here connected with the Government is lifeless, soulless, and impersonal. The men mean well, though, under the circumstances, well doing is a near approach to the impossible.

Away down at the roots of the mountains are the village officials, who believe it to be their business to put the best possible face on everything, and to conceal all that is vulgar or distasteful from the secretariat. Knowing what will please Simla, they do their best to supply what is wanted. From the low-paid venal village police officials, the report goes to the superior officers, from the superior officers to the district collector, from the district collector to the Provincial Government, and from the Provincial Government to the Imperial. In the course of this process of transmission much sifting and refining goes on, and woe betide the district officer who dares to allow his own opinions to obtrude themselves unduly, even in matters of fact! I had cases quoted to me in which such men had been victimised for daring to say that there was a famine in their district when the Governor of the province had said that there was none. The collector is the man in whom everything is focussed. He is head of the police, magistrate-in-chief, chairman of the District Board, and half a score of other things. No human being could perform all the duties imposed upon the District Collector and give them that personal attention which is so necessary if the human touch is to be maintained. For a quarter of a century it has been recognised that a state of things inaugurated by John Company a hundred years ago has outgrown its usefulness and requires changing. Lord Ripon recognised this as long ago as 1884, and tried to introduce drastic changes. One thing he urged was that magisterial and administrative functions should be separated, since it is obviously absurd that the official responsible for framing a charge should also be the party to try it.

The Viceroy has a legislative council to assist him, in which there are some elected members, all the rest being officials or nominees. All measures, including the Budget, require to come before this council. In the discussion of the Budget, each member is allowed to make one set speech, but may not move any amendments, or reply to any official statement. This, needless to say, is a mere caricature of discussion. No member may introduce a Bill without first obtaining the leave of the Government, and, so far as I was able to ascertain, no such permission has ever been granted.

What is true of the central government is equally true of the provincial ones, all of which are modelled on similar lines. The amount of interference from provincial headquarters with the management of purely local matters has to be seen to be believed. Since Lord Ripon's days there has been a certain amount of popular municipal government in the principal towns, though the system varies in different provinces. The municipal boards are partly elected by the people with the addition of nominated members. In some cases the nominated members represent one-half the number, but the general rule is the other way. These boards have charge of sanitation and other matters pertaining to the town, in theory at least. In actual practice they dare not spend one pie (which is the twelfth of a penny) without permission from the provincial Government. I had one case given me in which the town clerk of a big city had spent fourpence on a note-book, and the amount was disallowed because authority had not been obtained from the Government beforehand. At Madras, the municipal board proposed to raise the wages of some of its employees by one rupee, that is, 1s. 4d. per month. The Government, however, disallowed the amount, and only gave way after a considerable rumpus in the municipal board itself, which was unanimous on the proposal.

I attended one meeting of a District Board in Southern India. These District Boards in the South are elected from the Taluq Boards—say Rural Councils—which are themselves nominated by the Collector, so that here the element of popular election does not come in. These District Boards are also subjected to the same restraints and restrictions as the municipal boards. There was a case illustrating this at the meeting which I attended. District Boards have not only control over roads and other like matters, but are also empowered to build railways, and the Board in question had been particularly successful in this latter field of activity. For two and a half years the Board had been in conflict with the Government anent a proposal to build a branch line to open up a portion of the district. When I say "the Board" I mean the Collector, as I shall show later on. In the end the Government had granted permission to the Board to build the railway, but insisted that the rails used should be 40-lb., whereas the Board wanted to use a 56-lb. rail. This the Government would not permit, and insisted not only on the 40-lb. rails being used, but also on the line being constructed by the engineer of the South Indian Railway Company. Former lines had been constructed by the engineer of the District Board, and there was no charge against his competency or ability; but on this occasion he was imperiously set aside in the interests of the engineer of a private concern.

The strange fact in the situation was that at that very time the South Indian Railway Company was itself tearing up its 40-lb. rails and replacing them by the 50-lb. standard. It was openly alleged by responsible local officials that the Government of Madras and the South Indian Railway Company between them had a large stock of 40-lb. rails, and the Government having reluctantly given its consent to the construction of the proposed district line, was seizing the opportunity which the new line offered of "dumping" down its old useless stock on the district. Be this as it may, the Government decision came before the Board meeting, and the Collector, who presides at all these meetings, announced that the Board had better agree. He himself was against the 40-lb. rails, and thought it would seriously interfere with the prospects of the railway, but the Government had decided the matter, and, after all, the Board would have an opportunity of reconsidering the point thirty years after, when the rails would require to be relaid! Round the Board table were some thirty intelligent Taluq Board representatives, many of them landowners of good social position, and all of them opposed to the Government proposals, as was also the engineer and the bulk of his fellow-officials, and not one of them raised any objection to the course advised by the chairman. They would have been equally unanimous had the Collector taken the other side, and gone against the Government. Subsequently, I inquired of some of them the reason for their silence, and was informed that there was no use saying anything against the Collector's opinion, since if they did so they would be held to be obstreperous members, perhaps be charged with sedition, and for a certainty would not again have been nominated to the Taluq Board.

This, then, is the system of government which obtains—bureaucracy at the top and bureaucracy all the way down. In this connection I may add that the first draft of the so-called reform proposals sent out from the India Office would only have perpetuated and aggravated the existing system. The landed aristocracy and gentry were to be called in as advisers to the Viceroy, whilst such limited powers of popular election as are now possessed by the poor were to have been curtailed. No one alleged that the system of popular election for local boards in Bengal, where it operates in the country districts as well as in the towns, had worked badly; yet the proposals aimed at taking from the poorer classes such rights of popular government as they at present possess, and conferring new and extended rights on the aristocracy and landed gentry. Fortunately these have now been withdrawn and others more in accordance with real forward progress have been substituted.

It came upon me as a surprise to learn that the Viceroy has no Indian secretary. The present Viceroy, Lord Minto, has won golden opinions for his courtesy and his kindliness of disposition, and his very evident desire to ease the strain which exists between the educated Indian gentlemen and the Anglo-Indian officials. His principal private secretary is also a man of first-class ability and urbane demeanour, a remark which applies equally to his assistants. But after all this has been said, the fact still remains that the situation might be greatly improved if the Viceroy had as one of his secretaries an educated Indian gentleman, who would understand the people and their claims, and give a sympathetic interpretation to their grievances. Surely this small concession to Indian opinion might well be inaugurated during Lord Minto's reign, and the fact that one Indian gentleman now finds a seat on the Viceroy's Executive Council encourages the hope that an Indian Assistant Secretary will follow.

Such, then, is the Government of India, bureaucratic in form, and, as a consequence, harsh and exacting in all its relations towards the people. To the heads of departments the people of India are but so many seeds in an oil-mill, to be crushed for the oil they yield. It may be that all the provinces of India are not yet fit for the colonial form of self-government, but between that and the present soul-less bureaucracy there are many degrees of expansion in the direction of modifying bureaucratic power and enlarging the rights and liberties of the people. Sooner or later a beginning must be made towards enfranchising the masses and opening up the way for the educated Indian to fill the higher and better paid positions. A native head of a department would be more in touch with the people than an Englishman, and less easily imposed upon by the lower paid officials, and would generally make for the better government of the country. It may be seditious even to suggest such a thing, but it must not only be suggested, but pressed, if India is to be pacified and kept loyal to the British Raj. The framework of popular government is there, and it is only necessary to clothe it with the flesh, and breathe into it the spirit, of effective popular control.

NATIVE STATES.

There are in India about 300 states, with a population of 60,000,000, which are still under native rule. The late Lord Salisbury and other responsible statesmen have laid it down as an axiom of political wisdom that everything possible should be done to encourage the maintenance of the Native State. He it was who insisted on the restoration of Mysore after a British occupation of fifty years during which everything that ingenuity could do was done to make the return to native government as difficult as possible.

In each of these Native States there is a British Resident, who looks after British interests and keeps a watchful eye upon the estimates. Each state is under obligation to maintain certain military forces which are at the disposal of the British authorities when needed for the defence of India. This had its origin, I believe, in a good-natured offer on behalf of one of the Indian rulers at a time when there was threatened trouble with Russia, and what was then a voluntary offer of help on his part to the Imperial Government has become practically a compulsory charge on the Native States for all time to come. It hampers the Native States seriously in many directions; and surely, now that the menace, or alleged menace, from Russia, has been removed, this impost upon the Native States might well be discontinued. An Imperial Transport Corps, a company of Imperial Lancers, and certain military buildings are amongst the requirements, and as all of these have to be paid from state funds and yet are kept solely and exclusively for the use of the British Government there is a great deal of discontent concerning this obligation. I was only able to visit two of these states—Baroda, which was never under British rule—and Mysore. The Gaekwar of Baroda is a man of extraordinary energy and ability. He stands no nonsense from outsiders, as Lord Curzon learned to his cost whilst Viceroy of India. In Baroda reforms have been and are being enacted which destroy the whole thesis upon which British rule in India is supposed to be based. Take, for example, the caste system. In the State of Baroda education is free and compulsory, and applies to every caste and creed. Not only so, but special provision is made whereby 10 per cent. of the minor offices in the Civil Service of the State are filled by children from the lowest castes. The Gaekwar himself has set the example of mingling with all classes, and at a garden party given in my honour there were Hindus, Mohammedans, Parsees, and Christians, all mingling together on the most friendly terms. The Gaekwar is a Hindu, but his second Chief Justice in the High Court is a distinguished Mohammedan.

Popularly elected self-government is the rule in the towns and villages, and a Legislative Assembly has recently been created. The administrative and political functions have been separated, a reform recommended by a minute of the Viceroy's Council for British India as long ago as 1884, but which still remains a dead letter.

The other State was Mysore. Here, also, education is free and compulsory, and during my visit a lady was there who had been specially brought from London to give advice concerning school gardening, and an expert from Germany had been brought to teach the Sloyd system. The principal towns are lit by state-owned electrical plant, the power being derived from waterfalls and transmitted over ninety miles to the Kolar goldfields, also within the State. The whole of this great engineering undertaking was conceived and carried through by the late Dewan Sir K. Seshadri Iyer. For nearly thirty years a popular representative assembly consisting of 277 elected members has met annually in the capital of the State to discuss and recommend legislation, and the result has been that popular grievances have been ventilated and a most effective training for public life given to men of all classes. I understand that now the assembly has had legislative powers conferred upon it. In addition to all this three lakhs of rupees are set apart each year from the state funds for city improvements, and great wide streets are being cut through the old congested areas and sanitation is being attended to, and this not merely in the European quarters, as is the case in British territory, but in native quarters as well. Altogether the management of both these States is conducted on the most enlightened lines. I mention these facts to emphasise the argument which I maintain, namely, that given proper and sympathetic treatment the native population of India, at least in the South, East, and West, and as far North as the Punjab, is capable of a measure of self-government which would not materially differ from that which obtains, say, in South Africa or Canada. I am not arguing, nor have I ever done so, in favour of a uniform system for each province. In Canada and South Africa each of the separate States or provinces has that peculiar form of government which best suits its requirements, but the general principle underlying all the varying forms is that the people shall have effective control over their own affairs. If native States can provide free compulsory education, including technical training for all their children, can give popular government, popularly elected councils to the towns and villages, and have a popularly elected State Assembly, and generally conduct their business in a way which would bring no discredit to any country in Europe, surely British territory, with all the alleged blessings which British rule and tradition bring, should not lag behind. If those parts of India which for over one hundred years have been under British rule are not fit to be trusted with self-government, whilst those native states which have never been under British rule or which have shaken themselves free from it are governing themselves on democratic lines; and if the peoples inhabiting the native states and those in British territory are one and the same, surely this constitutes a sad reflection on British methods. The real facts are that the people of Bombay, Madras, Bengal, the United Provinces, and the Punjab are, if anything, even better fitted for self-government than are many of the native states, but to admit this would be to destroy the underpinning upon which British supremacy rests. I am not arguing for the withdrawal of the British from India, nor did I find any responsible exponent of Indian opinion who desired this. What I am trying to convey is that the people of India are fit to be trusted with such a large measure of self-government as would give them effective control over their own affairs and generally reduce British interference to the same limits as are exercised over the colonies in Australasia or South Africa.

POVERTY AND PLAGUE.

To understand the condition of the people of India it is necessary to keep one fact constantly in mind. That fact, given on the authority of Lord Curzon when he was Viceroy, is this—that the *average income of the people of India is only two pounds per person* per annum. This includes the incomes and salaries of rich and poor, official and non-official. The corresponding figure for other countries is:—

Russia	£11 per head
Germany and Holland ...	22 " "
France	27 " "
America	39 " "
England	42 " "

Mr. William Digby—no mean authority—estimated the income of India to work out at only £1 5s. 1½d. a year per person. But even accepting the higher official estimate, it is easy to see that in a country where the income of the people is less than one-fifth that of Russia, itself a poor country, and less than one-twentieth that of England, perpetual poverty is bound to be the lot of its inhabitants. Separating the peasants, who form 85 per cent. of the people, from the business and official classes, their income works out on Lord Curzon's official estimate at 26s. a year, or 12s. 6d. a year on the lower non-official one.

Of late years plague, famine, and pestilence, have stalked through the land, carrying death and destruction in their wake. The authorities are at their wits' end to account for the persistent prevalence of plague, which seems to have come to stay, and are scouring the laboratories of the world for a serum which will exterminate the plague bacillus. They are also making war on rats (which, it appears, carry the plague from village to village), and like famous Dick Whittington, are introducing ship loads of cats to exterminate them. After a hundred years, more or less, of prosperous British rule, during fifty of which Parliament has been kept annually informed, mainly in glowing terms, of the "material and moral progress of India," it is a trifle annoying to find that people die of plague and famine even more persistently than ever. But for the rat, and the flea which torments him, and which, so it is said, is the real disseminator of the plague, I know not what the British administrator would do. So long as he has the rat and the flea to fall back upon, his reputation as a heaven-sent administrator is safe. Having conquered all the other enemies of peace and order in India, he has but to prove his metal, or poison, against the rat and the flea, and peace and health and plenty will reign, and the brightest jewel in the British crown will shine flawless. Such appears to be the theory; alas for the reality!

If only one could shut one's eyes to facts, this rat-and-flea theory would be very comforting. It appears, however, to be the fact that rats and fleas were not introduced into India by John Company or his successors, and that, despite their presence, and without the aid of serum, plague did not persist then as it does now. In forty years—1860-1900—thirty millions (30,000,000) of people died of hunger in India—that, too, under the benign rule of the British Raj. What number died of disease in the same period will never be known, but all are agreed that the plague is now persisting and continuing in a way and manner hitherto unknown, and I believe the cause to be the *growing poverty of the people.*

I have read Lord Curzon's famous defence of British rule and of its beneficent influence upon the condition of the people, and have listened to much talk on the same subject, backed by official tables and percentages, without being convinced. That the condition of the peasants was ever worse than it is now is difficult to believe; that it was much better at no very distant date is, I am convinced, true. That the native rulers extracted all they could, and often much more than they should, out of the people is certainly true; that their methods were often the reverse of gentle is also true; but that they were able to apply the scientific methods of precision now in force for extracting the last pie from the peasant, and keeping him in abject poverty all the time is equally not true.

For one thing, the machinery did not exist for

doing so, whilst the methods then in vogue had a certain crude human elasticity which made it impossible. Under native rule the peasant's rent was not a fixed money payment, but a certain portion—one-third or one-fourth—of his crop. When the harvest was poor, the ruler's share of it was small in proportion. Each village had its panchayet for the settlement of disputes, and its council for all that pertained to its government. As has often been pointed out, kingdoms waxed and waned in India; one wave of invasion followed another; dynasties were established and overthrown with scarce a ripple of the surface of village life. Each village was a little self-contained, self-governing republic, which, so long as it paid its tribute in meal and malt to the ruling chief, was rarely interfered with. It had its own officials, full control over its lands; and even to this day the Government of India has hesitation in treating land as personal property, so firmly was the idea of its common ownership rooted in the popular mind. The peasant had the free use of pasture land for his cattle, was free to cut fuel from the forest, and was free to fish the streams and rivers all around. He did not require to dance attendance on half a score of officials and grease the palms of their underlings. If he required a new plough he cut the wood for it, and had it fashioned by the village carpenter, who was also paid in kind. When there was a full crop he had his straw or clay binns, in which he stored away the surplus, against the lean years of famine, and custom had established his claims to certain perquisites in connection with festivals, or on the occasion of a birth, a marriage, or a funeral in his family. He and all his relatives lived *en famille*, as they still do in the country districts, and the family was itself an integral part of the larger family which composed the village. Nor were the interests of the Pariahs so much neglected as it is customary to assume. Here, also, custom secured for the lowest class of workers, not only certain harvest perquisites, but also the free use of certain lands. It is sometimes thrown as a taunt at visitors to India that people who have spent a life-time there know little of the people, and for a mere globe-trotter to pretend to know anything is mere ignorant presumption. I was the guest of a missionary in a southern province, and was putting forward the view that all classes were worse off now than formerly. He agreed generally, but entered a caveat in the case of the pariahs. He had a good many of these under his training and selected some twenty of them, bright, active lads, to appear before us to get their version. They were unanimous in saying that things were worse for their class now because they no longer had the free use of land. The incident is instructive in more senses than one. A man may spend a lifetime in India and yet overlook some of the most obvious facts connected with the life of the people.

Nor were the ruling chiefs so remiss in their duties as it is now the fashion to pretend they were. To this day are to be seen, though often in disgraceful disrepair, the great tanks and waterways for irrigation purposes, carried out by these same native chiefs. Much boast is made of what is being done by the British in the way of irrigation; hitherto, beyond a number of great dams and canals, some of them marvels of engineering skill, the most that has been done has been to repair and improve the works which were there hundreds, probably thousands, of years before the conquering white man set foot on Indian soil. I have no wish to minimise all that has been and is still being done by the British Raj to introduce a settled form of government in India, but we must not overlook the fact that there is another side to the picture, and that the main concern of the rulers of India is not the improvement of the condition of the people, but the increase of the sources from which revenue can be drawn.

In saying this I am not imputing evil motives to the men who rule India, but simply stating a fact which, in my mind, admits of no dispute.

I conclude, then, that there is abundant evidence to justify the belief that the condition of the Indian peasant has worsened under British rule. The environment which for centuries had protected him has been shattered, and as a consequence he is less able to protect himself and his interests. New and strange conditions of life and government, in the control and direction of which he has no longer part or lot, have been forced upon him. He finds his poverty deepening and the burden of life pressing with increasing weight upon him, and not only is he without means of resistance, but he has no organ through which he can voice his woes. One answer to this is to quote the estimates of people killed by internecine warfare in the days of pre-British rule; but to this the retort has been made that all the wars of the world since the Fall of man have not destroyed so many lives as famine has done in India during the past half-century.

Plague then is, in the main, due to hunger, and that is a condition of things for which our system of governing India must be held directly responsible.

BRITAIN AS ABSENTEE LANDLORD.

For further proof of my contention that the lot of the peasant has worsened under British rule, let us consider his present condition. His rent is a fixed quantity, payable in coin, not in kind, whether the crop be good or bad. In wet lands, *i.e.*, irrigated lands, if there is no water and no crop no rent is charged, but if there is a one-anna crop—and a twelve-anna crop is reckoned the average, sixteen annas being a pukka or bumper crop—the rent to the Government must be paid in full. For the past ten years only three have been average years, all the rest being under. As the rent or revenue, as it is called, is fixed on the assumption that the yield will average twelve annas (that is, twelve annas to the rupee) a year, it requires no great stretch of imagination to see what this means to the peasants, who, even at the best of times, are always at close grips with poverty, with hunger only one degree, and not always that, removed from them.

When the peasant wants fuel he has to go to the Government depôt and buy it, or obtain a licence, on payment of a fee, of course, to go and cut it, even when the trees grow on his own land!

Before he can catch a few fish for his own and his children's supper he must take out a licence. The pasture land on which his cattle formerly grazed is now being enclosed as forest, and he has often to go long distances to find pasturage, and then has to pay. If one of his beasts should stray within the *unfenced* area of the forest it is liable to be impounded and he himself fined. Wild pigs and other animals may root up and otherwise destroy his crops, but he is not allowed to carry a gun to frighten them away. He is usually up to the neck in debt to the money lender, who claims a lien upon the crop ere it is reaped, the railway system giving facilities for having it carried to market. Thus the binns in which the surplus grains were formerly stored now stand empty or have totally disappeared. If his irrigation system is out of order, he is bandied about from one official to another to find out who is responsible, since, incredible as it may seem, in almost every department there are several sets of officials, each acting independently of the other.

As already indicated, the subordinates of each of these departments require to be bought off, and woe betide the luckless tenant who fails to stump up properly. If the ryot wishes to see an official he has often to walk miles to the nearest district office, wait there for hours, and then probably learn that he has gone to the wrong place. He will often spend days in this fashion, and only too often all to no purpose.

The Indian peasant is often sneered at as being unprogressive and shiftless. But what incentive has he to be diligent and active? Strive as he may, he realises that in the end the Sircar's kist will swallow up everything, and as he feels the weight of one impost after another weighing him down, and one restriction after another hemming him in, little wonder that his inherited fatalism comes to his aid, and he lets things drift, feeling it to be helpless to try to do battle against the tide which is carrying him forward towards the abyss.

As with the peasants, so, too, with the landlords where these exist. They are made to feel in a score of ways that their presence is an offence to a Government which exists for the "protection of the people," and so they are subjected to all sorts of imposts and restraints. They are forced to give terms and conditions to their tenants which the Government steadily refuses to those ryots who hold land direct from itself. Government officials tell of the exactions which the zemindars take from the ryots, and how but for the intervention of the Government they would make the lot of the peasant unendurable; and yet, strange as it may appear, I did not meet a single case of a cultivating ryot, and I met hundreds of them, who did not prefer to hold his land from a zemindar rather than hold it direct from the Sircar. There is a human element present in the one case which is wholly absent in the other.

The real rat plague, then, in India, is poverty, and the flea which spreads the disease is the Government. The emaciated, bloodless body of the ryot has no plague-resisting power, and so the fell disease finds him an easy victim. With more physical stamina he would have more power to resist, and the disease would die out. The Government and its officials all over the land battle manfully against plague and famine when these become acute; on that score there is no complaint against either their zeal or their humanity. What is overlooked, however, is the fact that the system now at work produces the conditions which make plague and famine inevitable; it, as it were, tills the soil and sows the seed of which plague and famine are the harvest.

And yet all might be so different. This country, so richly endowed by nature, and blessed with a population whose wants are few and easily met, might be made the garden of the world. Everywhere these kindly, simple people are full of discontent; they find themselves in the grip of a set of circumstances which they do not understand and which they cannot break through. Turn which way they will they are hemmed in by poverty, by restraint, which they did not create and which they are powerless to remove. The higher placed officials whom they have to meet occasionally are men of an alien race engaged in the performance of a more or less irksome task, and to whom each complaint means a fresh duty. The peasant is a poor, unlettered, half-naked, half-starved, and, in their presence, cringing being. He knows what he wants, but how is he to make his wants known to the strong, clean-limbed, well-fed, well-groomed, well-educated official who only imperfectly understands his language, who knows nothing, or next to nothing, of the conditions of his life, and who sees in his petitioner only a fresh cause of annoyance in an already overworked official life?

By one means or another the peasant must be given a corporate organ through which he can make his complaints manifest; must be given some effective control over the affairs which concern him; must be given some hope and assurance that if he exerts himself and seeks to improve his position, his efforts shall not end in being turned into a reason for still further adding to the kist of the Sircar. What I say of the ryot applies to the weaver and the artisan also, though if the peasant could be put well on his legs, that of itself would go a long way towards helping all the others. Meantime, amongst the many hapless poor whom commercialism is crushing into a shapeless mass, there are few more helpless than the patient, voiceless Indian ryot, with his one scanty meal a day, which in times of famine becomes no meal.

THE COLOUR LINE.

On November 9th I attended a King's birthday party at Tanjore Castle. I had visited the building in the morning, and been depressed by its dilapidated grandeur; and having another appointment there in the evening, I had not intended attending the party in the afternoon. For reasons, however, which need not here be mentioned, I looked in on the party for half-an-hour, and listened to the band and watched a score or so of white people enjoy themselves. The party, be it remembered, was a King's Birthday party, was given by the Ranee, widow of the late ruling chief, and attended by the two young princes. Apart from these latter and the servants, I saw no Indians present, and was subsequently told that the King's Birthday party *for the natives* would be given next day.

When I entered the train at Madras there were two Indian gentlemen in the compartment. One of them rose as I entered, and said: "Shall we move to another compartment, sir?" I stared at the man, and asked whether he had paid his fare. "Oh, yes," he replied; "but English gentlemen don't as a rule like to travel with natives." Now

I knew that in parts of America the colour line was strictly drawn, but I was not prepared for this kind of thing in India. Here, be it remembered, is a people who have inherited a civilisation which was old ere the West had begun to emerge from savagery. Those who travel first or second-class are mostly men with a university education, and speak English fluently. Some of them are wealthy, and many of them are of ancient lineage and noble descent. And yet, travelling on a Government railway in their own country, they are treated by the governing white caste much as they themselves treat the poor outcast pariahs.

There are carriages labelled "Europeans Only"; there are others labelled "Females." At some of the principal stations the urinal, placed as these places usually are at home, is labelled "European Gentlemen"; whilst away out at the end of the platform is a corrugated iron structure labelled "Men" at one side, and "Females" at the other. Any poor scallawag in a white skin, even if travelling third-class, is a "European gentleman," whilst a titled Indian with a Cambridge degree, and perhaps the blood of princes in his veins, is only a "man," for whom the corrugated iron structure has to suffice.

I could fill a decent-sized volume with cases which the reader would find it hard to believe, illustrating the way in which the colour line is drawn.

Here is one: I breakfasted one morning in a Northern city with a young Mohammedan gentleman, of handsome, refined appearance, whose forbears had been rulers in the land, and had built at least one of the mighty mausoleums which travellers to the north of India make a point of seeing. He had been educated at Cambridge, eaten dinners, been called to the Bar in London—at the Temple, I think—and is now practising as a barrister. On his return from England he entered a first-class railway carriage in which were two Englishmen, and was at once ordered out—the compartment was not reserved—and in the end, for his own comfort, was forced to go out to escape the studied insults of his travelling companions.

Take another case, which is better known and more discreditable: An Indian gentleman, knighted by the late Queen Victoria, a Christian, and an active supporter of missionary work, happened to be travelling, and was joined at a certain station by his son—who, by the way, is married to an English lady of good position. The son is darker in complexion than his father, and when he entered the carriage where his father was one of the other passengers objected. The father pointed out that there was plenty of room, and that he desired that his son should be beside him. This was the response from one of the men wearing the King's uniform: "Look here, we tolerated you because you don't look so bad, but I'll be damned if we allow that black dog in beside us." Father and son went out, and one can imagine their feelings.

In every town and cantonment there is a club,

but I question whether in all India there are more than a score or two of Indian gentlemen who have been admitted to membership. In Madras the club stands in off the roadway in its own compound, and when an Indian gentleman has occasion to call to see a member he has to leave his carriage on the street outside the gate and walk on foot along the carriage drive to the entrance. No self-respecting Indian ever thinks nowadays of applying for membership in one of these clubs. The Indians are everywhere forming clubs of their own.

It is not only in trains and clubs where this spirit is shown; it manifests itself everywhere and in every direction. There are cases in plenty of men and boys being whipped on the highway and otherwise punished for not making proper obeisance when some petty Government official passed. In one case in the North-West an Indian gentleman of good position, an income-tax payer, had a case in the local court. During a pause in the business he approached the magistrate to ask what place his case occupied on the list, and for this "offence" was ordered to stand in the corner of the court with his *face to the wall* for three hours. In the same district where this took place Indians must take off their shoes when entering a Government office, and are not allowed the use of a chair unless they can show a special authorisation entitling them thereto.

We hear a great deal about the abuse which a section of the native press pours out upon the English —and some of it, in all conscience, is in very bad taste, and should be discontinued; but we hear nothing about the insult, abuse, and contumely poured out day after day by a large section of the Anglo-Indian press upon the educated Indian. When men are being reviled, insulted, mocked, jeered at, and misrepresented day after day, it is not to be wondered at that some of them seek to pay out their tormentors in their own coin.

Everyone admits that the estrangement between native and European is growing, and many and varied are the explanations put forward to account for the undoubted fact. In the days when railway and other means of travel were less complete than now, the officials were perforce more in touch with the people among whom they lived all the time. Now there is more European society than of old; an official also travels more, goes occasionally to a hill station, and in addition goes home every few years, and so does not feel the same need for making friends among the people. Formerly, also, it was customary for a man to remain for years at a stretch in one district. Then, also, the work was not so specialised as it has since become, and the district collector was more in touch with all that went on. Nowadays it is a rare thing for a collector to remain longer than three or four years in a district, which may be as large as Scotland or Wales, with perhaps ten times the population of either, and then he is moved on to another where he is a total stranger. The result is that he never gets in touch with the people or their needs.

Add to all this the fact that education is spreading among the Indians, who avail themselves greedily of every educational facility, that business is developing, and that the educated Indian feels his position more keenly than he did a generation ago, that he is still, for all practical purposes, shut out from the higher and better paid positions, has no effective voice of any kind in shaping the destinies of his country, and is treated as a pestilent fellow if he suggests that he should have a voice, and one sees grounds enough for the growing race alienation with its consequent unrest in India.

For let it not be forgotten that the Indian people are of the same Aryan stock as ourselves. Take a gathering of Indians. Remove their graceful, picturesque costumes, and clothe them in coat and trousers, wash the sun out of their skins, and then a stranger suddenly let down into the midst of them would have difficulty in saying whether he was in Manchester or Madras. This fact has a very important bearing upon the question of how far the Indian people can be trusted with the right of self-government.

For the moment the gulf between the British official and the Indian people is widening. I have fared sumptuously with princes, sat at the table and broken the bread of the educated middle-class, and munched grain with the ryots, and the uniform unvarying testimony has been the same in every case. The older generation of Anglo-Indian officials sorrowfully admit the fact, though they differ as to the explanation. Nor could I discern any signs of an immediate change for the better. The partition of Bengal not only alienated the Bengalees, but is regarded as an act of hostility by the Hindu population in every part of India. The treatment which is being meted out to Indians in British colonies, especially in Canada and South Africa, is also a running sore, particularly with the Mohammedans. Recent acts of the authorities, especially the deportation without trial of men of good social standing and position, against whom no charge could be formulated; the suppression of public meetings, the support given to corrupt and inefficient police officials, and the establishment of a secret police service, with its agents in every corner; the growing oppression of the ryots, and the supercilious way in which their claims for redress are met, are all tending to shake the belief which was formerly universal in the impartiality of British justice and the fairness of British administration.

The Congress reform movement in India is not only not seditious—it is ultra loyal. Part of it is extreme in its moderation, whilst the other part is moderate in its extremism. There are men in both sections who have grown grey in trying to win for their people some rights of citizenship, and who, until just the other day, found themselves apparently as far from the realisation of their hopes as ever. What wonder that some of them have become soured, and that they and many of the younger men are now advocating a more forward policy? There is no sedition worth mentioning in India to-day. What there may be ten years hence, unless there be a great change for the better, I would not like to predict.

What can be done to bring European and Indian into closer and more sympathetic relationship? A very little statesmanship, inspired by a very little sympathetic appreciation of the situation, could easily set things to rights. If the bureaucratic official view is allowed to continue to prevail, then the outlook will continue black. Centralisation and lack of effective popular local control are at the root of the trouble. If only the withering hand of the bureaucrat could be removed from the municipalities, that of itself would go a long way.

It is made a cause of complaint that the Indian has not shown any great capacity for government even in the municipalities, where he has had the chance. But what self-respecting man of strong convictions is likely to come forward to take part in the unreal deliberations of a body whose every decision may be upset by an official who is not even a member? If the Madras Corporation is not permitted to increase the salary of an underpaid workman by 4d. a week, of what use is it talking of municipal powers? At Bombay, where Sir Pherozeshah Mehta proved himself a man of mettle on the Corporation, the entire official influence of the city was openly and illegally cast into the scale against him to bring about his defeat. I know that the law is that officials shall not take part in elections, and that save in important matters municipal boards shall not be interfered with; but the law is one thing and the practice another.

Then every village should have its popularly elected council, to which should be restored the control of the village school, the village wells and irrigation tanks, the grazing lands, the supply of fuel, and other matters closely connected with the life of the people. Especially, make the village council responsible, as of old, for collecting its quota of revenue for the Government. Let these councils be elected on a broad popular basis, giving, if need be, proportional representation to Mohammedans and pariahs. Then let the Taluk Boards be elected by these, and the District Board by the Taluk Board, and that will work wonders. The change would not be great—simply the creation of a popularly elected village or parish council; but the whole would thus be based on popular election, and not on nomination, as is the case at present over the greater portion of India, and that would make all the difference.

I would also revert to Lord Ripon's proposal of 1884, that no collector or other permanent official should be chairman of any board. Let him and others be present as advisers, not as dictators. Finally, let the District Boards, singly or in combination, elect members to the Provincial Councils, and clothe these councils with living powers. Let certain matters be delegated to the councils, and then leave them free to deal with them. If it be thought that this would be dangerous, let it be borne in mind that the Governor of a province, as also the Viceroy, has always the power of veto in reserve.

The one thing I ask is that the people of India shall be made to feel that they are being trusted, and are not being regarded and treated either as incapables or rebels. They are neither the one nor the other. They are, if anything, too loyal; whilst their capacity as rulers and administrators is being proved in every direction.

One other reform I would suggest. Let the way be opened up whereby men of tried and proved capacity may be promoted from the Provincial Civil Service to the Indian Civil Service. It is monstrous that an Indian, no matter what his qualifications, who has not been able to visit London in order to pass his I.C.S. examination, should have nothing higher than a deputy collectorship or sub-district judgeship to look forward to, whilst an Englishman of perhaps inferior capacity, who has sat for a certain examination in London, may one day rule over a department at Simla, or even become Lieutenant-Governor of a province.

There is nothing wild or startling about these proposals, nor would they be difficult to realise if only the necessary spirit were there in which to approach them. But that spirit and influence must come from without; the bureaucracy, after the nature of its kind, is hopeless. The one way to break down the colour line is to raise the official status of the people. So long as they are being govered as a subject race, just so long will they be looked down upon by their rulers. Just so long also will men of education and ability feel the bitterness of the insult which their present position implies. In this, as in so much else, self-government is the solvent to which we must look for dissolving a difficulty rapidly becoming unbearable. Educated India, a small but growing proportion of the people, is realising the truth of Mill's dictum that such a thing as a government of one people by another does not and cannot exist. "One people may keep another for its own use, a place to make money in, a human cattle farm for the profits of its own inhabitants." It is this "cattle farm" method of treatment that educated Indians are revolting against; and thus there are tendencies on both sides which are broadening the colour line and leading to greater estrangement of the races. When Indian can meet European as a fully enfranchised equal, and compel that respect which is his due, then, and not before, will race prejudice begin to die out and finally to disappear. So long as India is held in subjection the growing alienation of the races is bound to continue with increasingly serious results upon the good government of the country.

RECAPITULATION.

EVERY Session Parliament gives one day, or part of a day, to the discussion of the Indian Budget. On these occasions the Secretary of State for India is able to paint the state of Indian finance in glowing colours. What is rarely hinted at is that hidden in the background lies the plague-stricken emaciated figure of the starving peasant, from whose ceaseless toil the taxes are extracted. The income of the peasantry, who form 85 per cent. of the population, has, as already stated, been variously estimated as ranging from 26s. per head per annum to as low as 12s. 6d. One spare meal a day is common over vast tracts of country, and even that is not always forthcoming. When it is borne in mind that the Budget surpluses are wrung from people in this condition, there is room for other feelings than gratification. The land revenue paid by the starving ryots has gone up from 229,000,000 rupees in 1888 to 304,000,000 in 1908, an increase of 32 per cent. in twenty years. Every new irrigation canal, or railway, is used as a further means of extorting more revenue, and is, therefore, of very doubtful value to the people. The famine area in 1908 spread over 133,000 square miles, and affected 49,000,000 people, a fact of itself sufficient to give our complacency pause. Military expenditure has been growing in India with alarming rapidity, and there is only a very modified hope that it will be reduced. During the last eight years the sum accounted for in the Indian Budget under this head has risen from just over £14,000,000 to £20,750,000 —an increase of £6,500,000. That in itself is a very serious item, and in my opinion accounts for much of the unrest in India. It is not merely the money to which I refer, but the growing spirit of militarism in the administration of the civil affairs of India which the increased expenditure upon the army implies.

Then in regard to education. It gives great satisfaction to every friend of India that the expenditure upon education is being gradually, though slowly, increased. The increase, however, is far from being sufficient to meet the requirements of the case. The educational needs of India are great, and the desire for the education of their children on the part of the ryots is one of the most cheering signs of the times. One of the sights which I never failed to see when visiting the villages away from the big towns, was the local village school. The parents of the children are charged fees which, considering their position, are considerable, yet those fees are paid cheerfully. The village schoolmaster, out of his fifteen rupees monthly salary, will sometimes pay the fees of children whose parents are too poor to pay them themselves, in order to enable the children to get the advantages which the village school affords. The Government, therefore, might well be more generous in its expenditure upon education and educational requirements. I say nothing concerning the quality of the education given in the higher grades; further than that I agree *in toto* with the criticisms as to its exclusively literary character. That criticism, by the way, applies to our own country as well as to India.

Unquestionably there is great need in India for a more all-round education than is at present given. One of the pathetic sights of India is to see its decaying hand industries. With a little encouragement from the Government, and with a little stimulus to education, most of these hand industries, which represent a phase of the people's life which should not be allowed to die, might be preserved, and a fair measure of comfort secured for millions of homes. It has been conclusively shown ,for instance, that in the production of cotton a weaver with a modernised handloom can hold his own against the steam power machine. I have already referred to what is being done for education in the native states of Mysore and of Baroda. These native states set an example which the British Government might well follow. Surely if we hold India for the good of the Indian people we should not be content to lag behind a small native state in the matter of education.

A great deal is being done by the Government of India to prepare in advance by means of relief works and other measures to cope with the ever recurring famines. This is good, but much still requires to be done to stay the ravages which plague and other diseases are increasingly making. An alarming feature of the outbreak of plague in recent years has been its continuity, and its increasing virulence. For the last decade of last century, 1890-1900, the average death-rate from this preventable cause was over a million a year, and during the eight years which have elapsed of the present century the death-rate has even exceeded that appalling figure. That is a very serious state of affairs. At Poona I found the plague being grappled with, in spite of the opposition of one of the chief officials of the district, by a joint committee of officials and Indians who volunteered to assist. The presence of the Indian gentlemen on the committee gave the poorer people a degree of confidence in the sanitary measures which is often absent owing to their not understanding them, or their want of confidence in the intentions of those who try to enforce them. The example is one which can be recommended to other parts of India.

We hear much of the causes of the unrest in India, but the real cause, though there are others which have contributed, is the hope deferred of the Indians. Time and time again they have had legislation passed and reforms promised, and some reforms the Viceroy or the Provincial Governor have done what they could to inaugurate. But over and over again the promise which has looked so fair to the eye has been blasted to the hope, and as a consequence we have this gathering volume of unrest in India culminating in those recent acts connected with bomb outrages, which every friend of India must deplore. If the new reform proposals, which we are told have the full approval and sympathetic support of the Indian Government, are so administered as to limit what the Under-Secretary described as "the excessive official interference" with the people, and to associate Indians more and more with the administration of their country, and generally, both legislatively and administratively, to bring the people more into touch with Indian affairs, unquestionably the dawn of a new and brighter era is about to break in that distracted country.

This, perhaps, is the proper place for dealing with a personal matter. I reached Calcutta on September 18th, 1907, and, as already stated elsewhere in this book, almost at once proceeded to visit the interior of Eastern Bengal. Calcutta one morning—on October 3rd to be precise—was astonished to find that, according to the London press, I had been preaching "sedition" in India and libelling the Anglo-Indian officials. Calcutta itself knew nothing about it, and until the news was telegraphed out from London neither the officials in Calcutta nor the able journalists who conduct the Anglo-Indian press there, were aware of what I was supposed to have been doing. What was the statement which appeared to set the heather on fire, not only in Great Britain, but, as I subsequently discovered, all round the British

Empire, and which still finds credence by members of the House of Lords and other ill-informed persons? The *Times*, in a leading article on October 2nd, 1907, stated that:

> "The Bengali newspapers assert that Mr. Keir Hardie has declared the condition of Eastern Bengal to be worse than that of Russia, and that the atrocities which *officials commit* there would cause more horror in this country, were they known, than the Turkish outrages in Armenia."

The pressman who had sent the cable through Reuter's Agency was challenged on the spot by five of his brother journalists, all Englishmen, and two of them Conservatives, to produce his authority for the statement. He was unable to do so. The statement was a pure concoction. The man who invented it had such a reputation for misleading the public at home concerning affairs in India that seven of his brother journalists in Calcutta, prior to this incident, sent a warning note to the editors of British newspapers to be on their guard against statements emanating from him. One or two of the home newspapers, when they found how they had been taken in, had the decency and the good taste to apologise for having assumed the statement to be true. But despite that, and although every schoolboy who takes an interest in politics is aware that the statement was a fabrication, certain journalists and others still continue to accept the unsupported testimony of this one discredited scandal-monger against the testimony of all the responsible authorities and journalists in Calcutta and other parts of India. I am prepared to abide by what the Viceroy and the India Office (where, no doubt, my sayings and doings in India are duly recorded and filed away) say in regard to my general conduct. I am not troubled about a personal matter concerning my own reputation, but when my alleged sayings are used to prejudice people at home against what I have to say about the people of India and their condition it becomes necessary to make the truth known.

There is one aspect of recent Indian Budgets which is a matter of great satisfaction and that is the decrease in the revenue from opium. At the same time there is a risk that the prohibition of the use of opium may encourage the use of other drugs of a more dangerous character. At Singapore, in company with Sir John Anderson, the Governor, I visited the opium dens, and saw subsequently morphia victims who were literally covered with sores from head to foot. These were men no longer able to buy opium, and their condition was in every way more loathsome and deplorable than that presented by the opium wreck. Therefore it is necessary for reformers to be on their guard lest in suppressing one evil they do not create an even greater one. Another matter of social importance is the increase in the revenue from the sale of liquor. During the past thirty years the increase has been £5,000,000, and appears to be still increasing. It has been said that this is a proof of the prosperity of the Indian people, but I cannot accept this theory. As a rule people do not drink to excess when they are comfortably off and well-to-do. It is when they are miserable that they try to drown their sorrows in liquor, and it is the case that those villages in India where the local toddy shops carry on the most successful trade are those in which poverty and destitution are without parallel in any part of the world. At Amampett, a small poverty-stricken village a few miles from Tanjore in Southern India, which I visited, there is but one toddy shop, but that yields the Government a revenue of some 1,000 rupees a year. The Rev. Herbert Anderson, who was at the head of a deputation which waited upon me in Calcutta, and who is the president of the temperance association there, stated that the revenue from the sale of spirits and liquors in Bengal for the year 1905-6 was £1,100,000, an increase of £73,000 over the preceding year. For all India the liquor revenue has gone up from £1,561,000 in 1874, to £6,000,000 in 1908. That state of things in a nation where the use of intoxicating liquors is condemned by all forms of religion is very serious. I agree with the suggestion made by Mr. Anderson that one necessary step to check this evil is to separate the revenue from the licensing function. At present they are both in one department, and, without maligning anyone, it naturally follows that the revenue officer is likely to be more active in increasing his revenue than in acting as a temperance reformer anxious to keep down drunkenness. The separation of those two departments would go a long way towards removing the pressure which is brought to bear in various ways to increase the sale of liquor in India in order to replenish the exchequer. The matter demands the serious attention of the Government both in this country and in India, and is one which should not be overlooked.

The need for great political reforms in India is a point which is no longer in dispute. Even the House of Lords and the *Times* now admit this. But if the proposed reforms are to effect their object they must be accompanied by other measures. The people of India have for the moment lost confidence in British rule. It is not disputed that much of the unrest is due to the way in which the partition of Bengal was brought about. Everybody now tries to evade responsibility for the act. Lord Curzon says it was forced upon him by the India Office, and Lord Midleton, who, as Mr. St. John Brodrick, was Secretary for India at the time, retorted that Lord Curzon insisted upon it, and the Indian Office agreed to it in order to humour him. The particular form of partition which was carried through was not only opposed by the Hindu population of Bengal, but also at its inception by the Mohammedan population and by the civil authorities. Surely there is here at least a case for inquiry. The only justification offered for the boundaries as they have been fixed is that the Mohammedan population are given a sphere of influence in Eastern Bengal where they are in a considerable majority, and that to interfere with the existing arrangement might give them offence. It is true that the Nawab of Dacca favours the partition, but surely it is not in order to conciliate him that offence is to be given to most other men of social standing in the province. The Government of India is not surely reduced to the necessity of offending the Hindu population in all parts of India in order to give the Mohammedans a semblance of power in a portion of one province. I have already, from my place in the House of Commons, appealed with all the power at my command to the Secretary of State for India not to consider this question a closed book. If partition is an accomplished fact, at least he should see to it that the boundaries are so adjusted as not to give unnecessary cause of offence to a population of loyal and law-abiding people. The scheme of partition agreed upon by the Civil Service in Bengal, and assented to by all sections of the people, does all that is necessary to bring administration within reasonable bounds and might well be reverted to.

Concerning political reforms, I am certain that no matter what is done for India there can be no real pacification, no allaying of discontent, no breaking down of the barrier rising between European and Asiatic, until the people of India have some effective form of self-government. In the civil departments the more highly paid positions are practically closed against the Indians.

There is not a single Indian employed in the salt department with a salary of over 800 rupees a month. The higher positions are all reserved for Europeans. In the Customs Department the line is drawn at 700 rupees. These figures were given by Mr. G. K. Gokhale in the Viceroy's Council in the Budget debate of 1905, in the presence of the Viceroy himself and his officials, and so far as I know have never been controverted. In the Public Works Department the maximum for Indians is 1,200 rupees. The natives of India are thus practically barred from the higher paid positions in their own Civil Service.

The following table, compiled from official sources, shows the way in which the higher paid appointments are reserved as the all but total preserve of young men sent out from England. The figures relating to salary are given in rupees, the exchange value of which is now 15 rupees to the (£) pound sterling. Further, Eurasians, or half-breeds, are classed as Europeans for the purposes of the table.

Salary.	Total Appointments.	Indians.	Europeans.
Administration.			
75-200 Rupees	5080	4699	381
200-1000 „	1989	1267	722
1000 & over „	707	16	691
Education.			
75-200 Rupees	3379	3286	93
200-1000 „	1494	805	689
1000 & over „	191	6	185
Customs.			
75-200 Rupees	1812	1219	593
200-1000 „	752	324	428
1000 & over „	—	—	37

The examinations for the Indian Civil Service are held in London, and an Indian who wishes to sit can only do so by incurring the enormous expense of travelling to England. Formerly Indian gentlemen of means undertook this burden freely and sat for examination with the view to obtaining these positions, but the number appointed was so very small that they no longer trouble to do so. They ask that simultaneous examinations should be held in India and in England—a very reasonable request. There is one reform which I would suggest as thoroughly practicable, and with which most people will be inclined to sympathise. There are two branches of the Civil Service in India—the Provincial and the Imperial. The lower paid positions belong to the former and the higher paid to the latter. The Provincial Service is mostly recruited from Indians, and the universal testimony is that they perform their duties efficiently and well. But, no matter what ability or capacity they display they can never rise out of the lower paid Provincial Civil Service. Surely it is possible to adopt a system whereby the Provincial Civil servants might, after a certain number of years' service, and after proving that they are qualified, rise to the higher service. That would give young men who are capable administrators something to look forward to. At present they know that once they enter the Provincial Service, the higher service is closed to them for all time coming.

In regard to the legislative and administrative councils, a very small change in the system by which members are appointed to these would bring them under popular control. It is a well-known fact that the Law Courts are becoming one of the most grievous burdens with which the people of India are afflicted. In saying this I am casting no reflection on the Courts, but stating a fact which everybody in India knows. The habit of going to law has become so prevalent, and the law's delay so costly, that the obtaining of justice has become a serious matter. Under the old condition of things each village had its own Panchayet and Council, which settled most of the disputes that now find their way into the Law Courts. These Councils still exist in some villages. The restoration of the old Village Council, on a popularly elected basis, and entrusted with certain well-defined powers in the trial of civil cases up to a certain amount in small petty disputes, would be a welcome change of far-reaching importance. These Village Councils should also, I repeat, have the control of the village school, irrigation, grazing lands, and woods and forests within their areas. The charges for woods, grazing lands, fishing licences, and this, that, and the other charge, did not exist until a few years ago. These charges are grievous in themselves, and it sometimes happens that a piece of land which from time immemorial has been grazing land is suddenly declared to be forest land by the Imperial Government, and people whose cattle stray thereon are fined for trespass. If these lands were restored to the Village Council the people would have a real interest in the administration of their own affairs. I have been blamed for saying that the peasantry of India in intelligence and in capacity for looking after their own affairs compare favourably with our agricultural population at home. I repeat the statement. They have no book-learning, they do not know much about Western science, but in all that affects themselves they have a shrewd practical knowledge which reminded me of the Scottish farmer at his best. They can be quite safely trusted with the administration of village affairs.

The system of local government varies somewhat in different parts of India. In the South and West there are Taluk Boards (or Rural Councils) acting under the District Boards, which are the chief administrative unit outside the big towns. The District Boards are composed partly of officials and partly of members nominated by the Taluk Boards, and are presided over by the District Collector. They have fairly extensive powers of administration. In the Madras Presidency the Taluk Boards are wholly nominated by the District Collector; in Bombay they are one-half nominated and one-half elected, and in Bengal the elected portion is two-thirds of the whole, and there the system works well. My suggestion is that the old village council, one of the most ancient and successful of Indian institutions, should be restored and be popularly elected by the villagers themselves. These Panchayets, or Village Councils, should elect the members to the Taluk Boards, who in turn should elect the District Boards, and these, in conjunction with the Municipal Councils in towns and cities, should send members to the Provincial

Councils. In this way the whole superstructure of Indian administration would rest upon popular election, and the people would be given a real control over their affairs. At present the Provincial Councils are practically passive, and members have no power even to move amendments on the Budget. Provided that enlarged powers are given to the Provincial Councils, the young men of India who are imbibing our Western ideas will have an outlet for their energies and scope for the exercise of their ability which will keep them out of the way of "wandering agitators" and other "pestilent and pestiferous persons."

It has been said that owing to the diversity of castes and creeds India could not work a system of popular elections. That statement is capable of easy disproof. At the present time in Bengal three-fourths of the members of the local councils are elected by popular vote; in the province of Bombay one-half of the members, whilst in that of Madras the whole of the members are nominated. In all the big cities and towns of India there are popularly elected town councils.

I could quote numerous cases to show that people of different castes and creeds unite at elections to secure the return of non-sectarian members to all elective positions. Let me give one illustration. The city of Benares is the holy city of the Hindus, and the facts I am about to state were given me by the town clerk, who is himself a native Christian. In that city there is not a single ward in which the Mohammedans have a majority of electors. There were, at the time of my visit, nineteen members who had been elected by popular vote to serve on the City Council. Of that number twelve were Hindus and seven were Mohammedans. Here, then, was an instance in which Hindus were voting for and returning Mohammedans. The same thing is to be found all over the country. In Madras a Provincial Council member was being elected when I was there. Madras is a Hindu province, 85 per cent. of its people being Hindus. The Hindu organisation had brought forward a Mohammedan gentleman who was subsequently elected to represent them. The talk about caste and creed in this connection is greatly exaggerated, and if it is desired to break down caste prejudices the best method is to give the people some form of popular representation in connection with which they would be compelled to work together as citizens for the common good.

The present moment is doubly serious for this country and its relations with India from every point of view. It is not merely that unrest is growing in India; unrest is growing throughout the whole of the East. There is a popular movement in Turkey which has compelled the Sultan to grant a popularly elected Parliament. In Persia there is a revolution in progress in support of a democratic constitution. There is the great awakening in Japan, and there is the development taking place in China. India, after all, has more affinity with the East than with the West, despite 150 years of European occupation. The

Hindus and Mohammedans with whom I came in contact were kindly well-intentioned people. The Hindus in particular are very much maligned, for if they have one fault greater than another it is their submissive loyalty. Those people, who are kindly-affectioned, well-meaning, responsive to sympathy, having no higher ambition in life than to live loyal under the British Flag, are being treated as pariahs. We have responsibilities not only to the people of India, but also in the face of Europe; for if unrest spreads throughout India a conflagration may one day break out in China, Japan, or even nearer home, which will set India ablaze and burn up the last vestige of British rule. The Indian people will be loyal if they feel that their grievances are being acknowledged and redressed; but repression of legitimate agitation, the confiscation of newspapers, the deportation without trial of their most respected and trusted leaders, together with a denial or postponement of what they have been led by proclamations by the Crown, by the promises of Ministers, and by Viceregal speeches in their midst to believe were their rights as British subjects, will produce that feeling of hopeless despair which breeds discontent and disloyalty and which will menace the safety of the Indian Empire. India a nation, is a growing sentiment, uniting races, creeds, and castes, and the British Raj would be well advised to recognise this portent ere it be too late.

FAREWELL.

There is more, much more, I would fain say, but time and space alike forbid. I would like to tell of the wonderful industrial arts of the people, of the sanitary condition of the European quarters of the towns, of the no sanitary conditions of the native quarters of the same towns and the villages, of the personalities in the Indian movement, of my own personal experiences of missionary work, of the educational agencies of both Hindus and Mohammedans, of the rapidly growing woman's movement, and much else.

At Tuticorin, where I took farewell of India, I was given a civic reception and send-off. A town's band and a native band turned out, and led a procession, in which was a long string of well-filled carriages, through the town, with police lining the streets. There were, I believe, thirty policemen on duty, and they lined two miles of streets! Little wonder some of them were perspiring towards the close. But it was the band that moved me most. When I arrived at the station it was turning out *My love she's but a lassie yet* in great style, though with many variations I had never before heard. As I walked across from the station to the hotel it gave us two staves of *God save the King;* and then—marvel of marvels—struck up the *Marseillaise.*

It was a fitting termination to a wonderful experience. In the hotel book at Tuticorin I inscribed a parody of Burns's *Highland Welcome:*

> When death's dark stream I ferry o'er,
> A time that surely shall come,
> In heaven itself I'll ask no more
> Than just an Indian welcome.

I was in earnest in thus expressing my feelings at the moment, and can now say honestly that—

> Time but the impression deeper makes
> As streams their channel deeper wear.

I went to India to see the people, and to learn of their grievances; during the two months I was there I mixed with the people, companioned with them, and found them sociable, trustworthy, and lovable. Their ability is not open to question. A great intellectual awakening is shaking this ancient empire to its foundation. A sympathetic interpretation of the facts will bind the people more closely to us and lead to their becoming a loyal self-governing part of the Empire. Repression will only intensify their determination to secure self-government, and may lead finally to the loss of what has been described as the brightest jewel in the British Crown. It is for statesmen to chose which path they will follow.

GARDEN CITY PRESS LIMITED, LETCHWORTH, HERTS.